TAKE YOUR SEAT AT THE Table

LIVE AN AUTHENTIC LIFE OF ABUNDANCE, WELLNESS, AND FREEDOM

ANTHONY ONEAL

NELSON BOOKS

An Imprint of Thomas Nelson

Published in Nashville, Tennessee, by Nelson Books, an imprint of Thomas Nelson. Nelson Books and Thomas Nelson are registered trademarks of HarperCollins Christian Publishing, Inc.

Published in association with The Bindery Agency, www.TheBinderyAgency.com.

Thomas Nelson titles may be purchased in bulk for educational, business, fundraising, or sales promotional use. For information, please email SpecialMarkets@ ThomasNelson.com.

Unless otherwise noted, Scripture quotations are taken from The Holy Bible, New International Version®, NIV®. Copyright © 1973, 1978, 1984, 2011 by Biblica, Inc.® Used by permission of Zondervan. All rights reserved worldwide. www.Zondervan. com. The "NIV" and "New International Version" are trademarks registered in the United States Patent and Trademark Office by Biblica, Inc.®

Scripture quotations marked NKJV are taken from the New King James Version®. Copyright © 1982 by Thomas Nelson. Used by permission. All rights reserved.

Library of Congress Cataloging-in-Publication Data

Names: ONeal, Anthony, author. | O'Neal, Sam, author.
Title: Take your seat at the table : live an authentic life of abundance, wellness, and freedom / Anthony O'Neal with Sam O'Neal.
Description: Nashville, Tennessee : Nelson Books, [2025] | Summary: "Are fears and uncertainties keeping you from reaching for your dreams? In Take Your Seat at the Table, bestselling author Anthony O'Neal reveals the indispensable tools and strategies to take ownership of your decisions and step into the life God wants you to live"-- Provided by publisher.
Identifiers: LCCN 2024027565 (print) | LCCN 2024027566 (ebook) | ISBN 9781400250066 (hc) | ISBN 9781400250080 (epub)
Subjects: LCSH: Christian life. | Peace of mind--Religious aspects--Christianity. | Well-being--Religious aspects--Christianity.
Classification: LCC BV4501.3 .O474 2025 (print) | LCC BV4501.3 (ebook) | DDC 248.4--dc23/eng/20240807
LC record available at https://lccn.loc.gov/2024027565
LC ebook record available at https://lccn.loc.gov/2024027566

Printed in the United States of America

24 25 26 27 28 LBC 6 5 4 3 2

To every individual who's tired of watching their life from the sidelines, ready to take the driver's seat and forge the life they are destined to lead. This one is for you!

CONTENTS

INTRODUCTION

O kay, Anthony, you got this."

I was pacing back and forth in my church office, trying to settle everything down before making the biggest presentation of my life up to that point. My office wasn't large, so my "pacing" was more like walking around in a little circle over and over. *Step, step, turn. Step, step, turn. Step, step, turn.*

"You got this, Anthony. You can do this."

My voice didn't sound nervous in my own ears, which was a good sign. But I sure felt nervous. Face flushed and warm. A few drops of sweat on my forehead and the back of my neck. Heart thudding. Stomach a little queasy.

"Uh-oh." Some kind of weird noise came rumbling out of my gut. A cross between a growl and a gurgle. Okay, maybe my stomach was *a lot* queasy! I hurried across the hall to the bathroom and sat down on the toilet for a few moments. Leaning my head into my hands, I had to fight against falling asleep. I'd been too anxious the night before to rest. After a few hours I'd gotten tired of just lying there on the bed, so I got up and practiced my presentation several more times.

Back in my office, I pulled the presentation up on my iPad for a final review. I was a youth pastor at the church, and I was about to join a meeting to plan a major youth conference for later in the year. If you've never been in youth ministry, you may not know those types of conferences are like the Super Bowl for youth leaders. They take a ton of planning and often require way more resources than a youth budget would typically include, but the returns can be huge. Teenagers coming to faith. Big connections being established. New families joining the church.

Those kinds of events can make or break a ministry, and I was determined for this one to be a success. I had all kinds of notes ready to go for my presentation. All the speakers I wanted to bring in. How I would make the best use of the church's multipurpose room. How I planned to maximize our connections with local high schools. All the steps I would be taking to manage the budget wisely.

This was my time to shine!

Pushing myself forward, I stepped out of my office and walked confidently down the hall toward the main conference room. I stopped outside the door just for a moment. One deep breath. Two deep breaths. A third to calm my nerves. Then I pulled the door open wide and went inside.

The senior pastor smiled when he saw me. "Anthony! Great timing. Come on over." He was sitting at the head of a large conference table in the middle of the room. Other staff members were seated around him, including the executive team and the chief financial officer. They were finishing up a separate meeting, and it looked like most of the people in the room would be staying to hear what I had to say.

There was just one problem: All the seats were taken. There were no empty chairs around the table.

A couple of other guys spotted the issue at the same time I did, and they kind of scooted back and gestured toward their chairs, looking at me with raised eyebrows.

"You want me to . . . ?"

"Should I . . . ?"

"Nah," I said, waving them back toward their seats. "I'm good."

I wasn't sure what to do, so I propped my iPad on a corner of the table and leaned against the wall opposite the senior pastor. Several people had to swivel in their chairs to watch me as I gave my presentation. Staff members turned toward me a couple of times to ask a question, then turned back toward the center of the table as they talked about my answer. I felt like I was on the outside looking in.

Overall, the meeting was a success. Everyone liked my plans, all the speakers were approved, and the budget looked good. I had done my job well.

Even so, I couldn't help feeling dissatisfied. This was my first time presenting to the executive team, and we were planning a conference where we expected thousands of young people to attend. This was a big moment, a huge opportunity—yet I couldn't even get a seat at the table.

What did that say about my role at the church? More importantly, what did that say about me?

A Little About Me

With the benefit of hindsight, I can look back and see how that whole situation was a perfect metaphor for my life. Not just for my life in that moment—in that conference room—but for everything I had experienced until then.

For years I had been standing off to the side while other people made plans for me. I'd allowed others to take the lead in my finances. In my physical and mental health. In my career, my relationships, and my dreams for the future.

I didn't have a seat at my own table. In fact, I'd *never* had a seat at my own table.

How did I get in that situation? The same way most people do. The only thing unique about my early story is that I have four parents. My mom and dad had me out of wedlock while they were engaged to be married, but they never got to the altar. My mom married an incredible man and eventually moved to California. My dad stayed in the Carolinas and married a wonderful woman. I hate the term *stepparents* and never use it, preferring just *mom* and *dad*. But for the sake of this book, I'll refer to them as my California parents and my Carolina parents. Amazingly, all four of my parents love me dearly, which I now understand is a rare privilege. I'm grateful!

Otherwise, my life was relatively normal in a solidly middle-class way. My California parents worked hard but didn't have a lot of money. I can remember using black tape to cover holes on the bottoms of my shoes because we couldn't afford new ones. I got a work permit when I was fourteen and took a job at Taco Bell on weekends and during the summer months. There were times when my mom would stop by and ask me to bring home something for dinner because we could use my discount.

Things got tougher financially when I got kicked out of school—twice. My mom quit her job to homeschool me. She turned our little kitchen table into the classroom, and overall we made it work. Our family stuck together and committed to pushing forward.

As I got older, I started to feel pressure from my parents to walk a certain path in life. They wanted me to go to college. I mean, they *really* wanted me to go. Neither of them had any education after high school, and they let it be known that a college degree was the key to a successful life.

"You need to graduate college, get you a good job, get you some real benefits—healthcare and a 401(k) and all that—get you a family, keep your head down for forty years, get you that gold watch, then retire. That's the good life."

That was the message I heard over and over. That was the plan for my life.

I did try to follow that plan—for a little while. I started college, but there was too much pressure to think a certain way. Too much freedom to avoid stupid mistakes. Too many stupid mistakes to stay out of trouble. When I dropped out, I made some poor choices when talking with my parents about my reasons. Said some things I never should have said.

That's how I found myself living on the streets in Southern California. Sleeping in my car. The rock-bottom moment came when I wrote some painful words on a piece of cardboard: PLEASE HELP. ANYTHING IS APPRECIATED. I sat down to beg on the same street where my mom and I used to shop for groceries.

It happened only two times, but those were the most humbling experiences of my life.

Thankfully, I eventually came to my senses and apologized to my parents. I got full-time work as a bill collector. Then a car salesman. Then I realized how many young people were in similar situations, which led me to start a nonprofit educating high schoolers on their financial futures. Which led me to become a youth pastor. By that time I had learned how to work hard, and I threw myself into those roles with discipline and intensity. I found financial success. It seemed like things were turning around.

But when I started making enough money to buy the things I'd always wanted and develop the lifestyle I'd always thought would satisfy me, I came to understand that everything I was doing primarily benefited people other than myself. I was working from sunup to sundown so my bosses would be financially secure or so my pastor could achieve his vision for his ministry.

My life was never about my dreams or my goals or my passions. It was never about my needs or my future.

Standing in that conference room, I did not feel worthy enough for a seat at the table because I was "just a youth pastor." Everyone else was more important, or so I thought. So I allowed myself to be pushed to the side.

Have you ever thought that way about yourself? *I'm* just *a . . . , I don't deserve to be here because I'm* only *a . . .* Those kinds of thoughts held me back for so long, and I imagine they might be doing the same thing in your life. That should not be so!

I'll never forget the day I sat down for an interview with

Success magazine. By that time I was working for Ramsey Solutions, which is an awesome company with an amazing mission to empower people to achieve their dreams. It was a great place to work during a pivotal moment in my life, and I loved the work itself. I got to launch my show, *The Table with Anthony O'Neal*, and be on the radio and TV, talking with real people about real problems and offering real hope. I got to create resources and write books. In so many ways, it was wonderful.

Then came the day of the interview. Dave Ramsey was the subject of the article, but the writer was also talking with the other personalities at the company, me included. The theme of the piece was *succession*.

The reporter was surprisingly direct. "You've spent several years now helping Dave Ramsey build his legacy," she said. "What are you doing to build your own?"

I knew the answer without even thinking: nothing. I was serving and doing good, meaningful work, but I knew I was capable of more. At some deep level, I knew that God had put a calling on my life that went beyond what I was doing—which meant I was still standing at the side of the table. Still afraid to sit down, or maybe still feeling unworthy of my own seat.

That was the moment everything changed.

A Little About You

I don't know the details of your story. I'm not sure if your experiences are similar to what I've just described or if your life has taken a completely different path. And you know what? It

Do you have the
ability to live
each day as your
authentic self?

doesn't really matter. The particular plot points of our stories aren't the main issue here.

The main issue is control. Do you have control over your own life? Do you have authority to shape your life the way you want it to be shaped? I'm not talking about "being your own boss" in terms of running your own business or having enough money in the bank to retire whenever you want or that kind of thing. I'm not talking about your money or your time or your career—not yet.

What I'm asking is whether you have the ability to live each day as your authentic self. To be the person you were designed to be and to pursue the purpose you were created to achieve.

I know these concepts may seem a little vague, so let me narrow the focus by asking three specific questions. First: *Have you ever felt pushed to the side of your own life?* I know many people who feel frustrated and angry about the lack of freedom in their lives. There's always someone telling them what to do. Where to go. What to say. What to think. Even who to be.

Freedom isn't just an American ideal. It's a necessary ingredient in the recipe of life. And we feel it when we don't have it.

Second question: *Have you ever felt weary from living at the bare minimum?* Maybe you have a financial issue. Maybe a relational one. Maybe your problem is connected to your health, whether physical or emotional. Maybe your career or your long-term goals need support.

Our culture has built itself on the promise of abundance. The American Dream. Life, liberty, and the pursuit of happiness. These are the prizes we've been promised all our lives. But have you received those prizes? Does your life overflow with blessings? Or do you find yourself looking for new ways to squeeze every dollar? Every moment? Every tender embrace?

Third question: *Do you feel unwell?* Yes, I'm talking about your physical health and well-being—at least to start. The modern world is producing unhealthy people at a staggering rate. Physically, we are exhausted. Addicted. Overweight. Overmedicated. We've lost our way when it comes to nutrition and balance and rest.

The same is true with our mental and emotional health. Not to mention our spiritual health, our financial health, and our relationships. Even our lives, on average, are getting shorter in this modern age. The world is chewing us up and spitting us out.

Does that apply to you? Are you unwell?

If those questions resonate with you—if the answer is yes or has been yes or is likely to be yes in the future—then I'm guessing you don't have a seat at your table. More specifically, you're not sitting at the head of your table. And that needs to change if you want to enjoy a life of abundance, wellness, and freedom.

The truth is, *many* people have been crowded out of their own tables. Maybe even *most* people. And it's killing us.

Imagine it this way: You're sitting off in the corner of your own dining room in your own house. In the center of the room is your family table—the one you picked out. The one you purchased and put together and arranged. Your dining room chairs are there, but they've all been filled with outsiders. Bankers are sitting at your table. And creditors. And politicians. And teachers. And your parents. And your bosses. And your neighbors. And your spouse. Even your kids.

Now imagine all those people deep in debate about your life. They're yelling and talking over one another. They're making plans and setting priorities. They're poring over every detail of your past and sketching out every moment of your future.

All the while, you're still in the corner trying to get a word in. "What about me?" You raise your arms and wave them back and forth, trying to grab somebody's attention. "What about what *I* want for *my* life? I have my own plans. I have my own dreams! Why won't you listen to me?"

Have you been there? Do you feel like you're there now?

A Little About This Book

The goal of this book is to show you how to take a seat at your own table. More importantly, my promise is to help you take a seat *at the head* of your own table. You can take control of your spiritual life, your physical and mental well-being, your career, your finances, and your relationships—and you can start that process today. Right now.

Why should you take your seat at the table? Because that's the only way to experience the kind of abundance, wellness, and freedom you've always longed to experience. That's the only way to step into the life you were created to live—a life of purpose and fulfillment.

I know it's possible because I've gone through the process of regaining my place at the head of my own table, and I've seen the results.

As I've said, being on a team with Dave Ramsey was an amazing opportunity that produced incredible results in my life.

I treasure the time I spent in that place and the lessons I learned from the people there. In fact, for years I truly believed working as a personality at Ramsey Solutions was the pinnacle of what I could achieve.

In my early thirties, I thought I had arrived. No more worlds to conquer. No more mountains to climb.

Thank goodness I was wrong!

In the years since I sat down at the head of my table, I've continued to speak on the big stages. I've been in the big publications. I've built a seven-figure business and sat at the table with some of the most successful organizations you can imagine. It has truly been a wild ride.

But the biggest benefit I've discovered is this: I get to be Anthony Bernard O'Neal. I get to live as my authentic self for every minute of every hour of every day.

I want you to know how amazing that feels.

You, too, can take your seat at the table. I know this is possible because I've had the privilege of helping many, many people do just that. These are people I encounter through my different businesses, including the Neatness Network. These are people I engage with on my podcast. These are people I live with and work with each day, including my team members.

Over and over I've seen this principle play out: Whenever people regain their proper place at their table, the floodgates open for abundance, wellness, and freedom.

That's my hope for you. That's why I've written this book.

As we work through these pages together, we'll start in chapter 1 by defining what I mean by *your table*—what it is, what it's made from, and how it applies to your life. Then we'll take a deeper look at what it means to sit at the head of your table in chapter 2.

Chapters 3 through 8 are the meat in the middle. They'll give us a chance to examine the specific elements of your table, which include your spiritual life, your mental and physical health, your work, your financial situation, and your relationships. Just as importantly, these chapters will show you how to bring the people to your table who can help you maximize those resources. Then, to close, chapters 9 and 10 will focus not only on keeping an open table that can adapt and grow but also on the importance of authenticity when it comes to operating at your table in the messiness of everyday life.

These precepts have changed my life. They've helped change the lives of many others. And I believe with everything I am that they can change your life as well. They can bring you to abundance, wellness, and freedom like you've never experienced.

Are you ready to take your seat at the table?

If so, let's go!

CHAPTER 1

DEFINING
YOUR TABLE

It seems like I've been sitting at tables pretty much my whole life.

When I was growing up in California, our family had a little wooden table pushed up against the wall in our kitchen. Five plain chairs around the edges. My Cali dad sat at the head of that table, facing the wall. My Cali mom sat on his right, with my sister, Yvette, next to her. My brother, John, and I sat on the other side of the table to the left of Dad. It's funny that even when we sat down at the table alone or in a smaller group, we always sat in the same spots—as if we had assigned seats.

In my family, everything happened around that table. We ate breakfast there to start the day, smelling my dad's coffee brewing a dozen steps away on the kitchen counter. When my siblings and I got home from school, we'd grab some Kool-Aid and slump down at the same table to do our homework (always in the same seats, of course). Then we'd have dinner, when everyone was expected to talk about whatever interesting stuff happened during the day.

We stayed in those chairs until we heard the magic words after eating all of our food: "You're excused." It was always Dad who said it.

We had family devotions at the table. We prayed together at the table. Mom always wrote up her grocery list while seated at the table, and I'd sit beside her and try to convince her to add some of my favorite treats.

Sometimes in the evenings Dad would yell out, "Kids, come to the table!" We'd come. We'd all sit together and wait for what was coming—usually a lesson Dad wanted to teach us, or sometimes a bit of news he and Mom needed to share. When it was good news, we celebrated together. When it was bad news, we cried together.

Always at the table. Always together.

When I was expelled from middle school, my mom quit her job and homeschooled me for a semester. Can you guess where we sat down together? Yep. She turned that table into a classroom. As soon as my brother and sister left for school, I was expected to have my butt in that chair and work. I didn't stop working until late in the afternoon when the bus went by and my siblings came running back into the house.

Most days I couldn't wait to jump up from that table to go outside and play with my friends. But I was always back at the same place and in that same seat come dinnertime.

When I left home, I thought I was leaving that table behind. Nope. Seems like most things I do in life, even today, I do around a table. I've got my own table in my own dining room now, of course. But even when I leave the house, I still find myself at tables of all kinds. Conference tables at work. Restaurant tables on dates. A custom-built recording table for my podcast.

Tables everywhere!

For me, those tables constitute a powerful picture of just about everything meaningful in my life. The table represents who I've been, who I am, and who I hope to be. It represents what I've experienced, what I'm experiencing now, and what I hope to experience in the future. The metaphor embodies me as a person *and* the most influential people connected to me.

I know you have your own experiences around the tables of your life. Your own memories and your own hopes. When you think about everything that happens around a table—all the joy and laughter, all the sadness and tears, all the boring little details of everyday life—it's pretty much a given that no two tables are the same.

So before we go any further, let's get on the same page. Before we dig deeper into what it means to take a seat at your table, let's take a little time to understand what the table is— and why it matters.

The Table Is Your Life

The first thing to know is that your table is your life. Your table includes the most important elements of who you are as a person and what you choose to do with your time, talents, and other resources.

So when I talk about taking a seat at your table, I am pointing to your life. I am shining a light on everything that works together to make you *you*.

Think of an actual table. Specifically, think of one of those farm-style tables you'd expect to see in a nice country home somewhere down south. Those tables aren't made from a single block of wood. Instead, they are formed by joining several long planks into a big, inviting rectangle. None of those planks is a table by itself, but each of those planks is *part* of the table. The magic happens when they all come together to actually form the table.

The same thing is true for you and your table. One of your planks, for example, is your physical body. Your skin and muscle and bone and brains. Your physical self is part of your table, which includes your physical health. Really, that's the most basic part of your table—that's where it all starts.

Your mental capacity is another plank in your table. Your mental health. The same is true for your spiritual side—your soul. That's the only part of your table that is eternal. Keep going down the list: your work, your finances, your possessions, your time, your family, your friends, and so on. Each of those things is part of you, which means each one is part of your table. Gathered all together, they make up your table, which is your life.

One more thing, and this is important: It's easy to visualize your table in terms of the present, which makes sense because you can only interact with your table in the present. But when you really think about it, your table is not limited to the current moment.

Your past is part of your table. The past includes all those experiences and memories that made you who you are. All those failures and lessons learned. All those triumphs and goals achieved. They're all part of you, which makes them part of your table.

Your future is also part of your table. Your legacy. That's because everything you do right now will impact your table in the future. Everything you build right now will define what you experience in the future. What you choose right now actually determines the dimensions of your table for tomorrow—and what you will leave behind for those who come up after you.

What is your table? It's your life. It's everything you've been given to manage within the boundaries of your existence.

The next thing you and I need to remember is that we've been given our tables for a reason. For a purpose.

Your Table Points to Your Purpose

I don't have kids yet, but I do have a niece and nephews. Man, it's a joy to show up at one of my siblings' houses and hear those little voices calling out from behind a window. "Uncle Anthony! Uncle Anthony!"

Usually I can see them jumping up and down before I even walk through the door.

Let me tell you something: When I visit my niece and nephews, I do it right. I show up with style! Uncle Anthony always brings energy and smiles and laughs. I run and play with those kids for hours. I ask them questions about their school and their friends and what kinds of mischief their parents are getting into. (Mostly joking there.) I yell when they yell. I jump when they jump. We plan out play fights based on their favorite superheroes. We get all riled up!

Then I go home and relax while their parents have to calm things down. Ha! The perfect plan every time.

One thing I've noticed about my niece and nephews is that they all go through a *why* stage. At some point, *why* is the only word that seems to come out of their mouths. "Why? Why? Why?"

We've been
given our tables
for a reason.
For a purpose.

I don't blame them! The world is a big place for little kids, and there comes a point in their development when they need to move beyond "What's there?" and start trying to figure out "Why is it there?" *Why* is a critical question for kids to carry in their pockets.

Actually, *why* is a pretty good question for adults as well. An important question—especially when it comes to your table.

Take a moment to ask yourself a couple of questions right now: Why does my table exist? Why do I have the resources and the experiences and the gifts that make up my life?

I can summarize the answer in one word: *stewardship.* Our lives are not our own, which means your table is not your own. My table is not my own. Each thing we currently possess or control was given to us by an outside source, and it was given to us with the expectation that we would manage it well.

We are blessed to be a blessing, as the saying goes (Genesis 12:2–3).

The sad truth is that most of us do a poor job of stewarding our lives. That was certainly true for me throughout much of my life. I was pretty selfish as a kid, and I carried that selfishness into adulthood. Everything I did was about me. Every goal I set was intended to benefit me. Every second I had was spent on me, every cent I had was spent on me, and just about every thought in my head was focused on me.

I remember the moment things started to change. At the time I was working as a bill collector in California, and I was good at my job. Work started at 5 a.m. so we could make calls to the East Coast starting at 8 a.m. I always showed up to the office at four thirty, ate a little breakfast, and then hit those buttons. Call after call. I put in more than my fair share of hours, and I earned my fair share of bonuses. After a couple of years, my supervisor told me I was about to be promoted, and I needed to train my replacement.

Sounded good to me!

I started that training the following Friday, which meant I needed to work through my lunch break. Now, back in those days, we used to get paper checks. First and third Fridays of the month. Usually, a group of us would head out to the bank over lunch and cash our checks—that way we were ready for the weekend. But because I worked through lunch, I just brought the check home with me.

That night, I actually stopped to look at my paycheck for the first time. I studied it for several minutes. It had the company name stamped on it in big, bold letters: DCB Associates. Those were the initials of the owner: DCB. I didn't have the words to express it at the time, but as I looked at that check, I felt like something was wrong. I had a fleeting understanding that I was giving away the best part of my time and energy every single day—not to build my own table but to build DCB. I was pouring myself out to build someone else's table.

That's when I heard the voice of the Holy Spirit in my heart. The voice of conviction: *It's good that you're using your gifts to help build your boss's vision. But how are you using those same gifts to build your own vision? What are you doing for AO Associates?*

In that moment, I began the process of realizing that I am made for something bigger than a paycheck. I was put here on this planet for more than filling up my belly with food or filling up my wallet with cash or filling up my mind with information.

I have a purpose.

So do you.

I like what my friend Dr. Dharius Daniels has to say on this subject:

> Your purpose is the unique contribution you are supposed to make on earth. The operative term is *unique*. You are not a carbon copy of anyone or anything. When God made you, God did it intentionally, not accidentally. He made you with an assignment in mind, and that assignment is to reform or change some things that only you can. So God designed you with destiny in mind. You can't allow the opinions of people to cause you to miss out on your assignment from God.[1]

I use that word *assignment* a lot because I think it adds a sense of urgency to the concept of purpose. I have an assignment. A mission. I wasn't created solely to enjoy myself or indulge myself. No, I was created to make a difference in the world. I was created to achieve something that only I can achieve.

The same is true for you. You have an assignment of your own.

Yes, each of us was meant to experience abundance, wellness, and freedom—and we're going to explore those values deeply and seriously throughout the chapters that follow. But it's also true that each of us was created *to help others* experience abundance, wellness, and freedom. That's part of our assignment. That's part of our purpose.

How do we do that? By doing a good job of managing our tables. By being good stewards of all the resources that make up our tables.

Remember, your table is your life—everything you've been given during your time here on earth. And the reason you've been given that table is to help you carry out your unique assignment. Your mission. Your purpose. Being a good steward of your table means maximizing all your resources in a way that brings meaning to your life *and* makes a difference in the lives of others *and* improves your corner of the world.

You know what? That's way too big a job to tackle alone.

Your Table Includes Your People

Here's a question: How often do you sit down at a table alone? Could be your own table at home. Could be a restaurant. Could be a conference table. How often do you find yourself sitting at a table by yourself?

I think that practice is becoming more and more common as our world becomes more and more isolated. Seems like I see it every day—a person hunched over a table in a coffee shop all by themselves, eyes looking at a screen and ears stuffed with headphones. Cut off from the rest of the world.

That can't be good for us in the long run. In fact, the second chapter of the Bible says, "It is not good for the man to be alone" (Genesis 2:18).

I don't say that to shame anyone. As a single person myself, I know how difficult it can be to feel lonely and isolated. I also know a lot of good things are at work in me right now, and I can accomplish a lot of good things in the world during this season *because* I'm single. Singleness can be a blessing when we approach it the right way!

No, I mention people sitting alone at tables because tables aren't really meant to be places where people sit alone. A table for one isn't a table—it's a desk. In just about every scenario, tables are meant for people, plural, to come together and connect. Dining tables. Conference tables. Ping-Pong tables. Even those little circular coffee tables have room for several people to put their drinks down while they chat.

In the same way, the table of your life needs people. Not just any people but those who play an active role in helping you steward your resources and carry out your assignment.

When I talk about taking your seat at the table, I don't mean taking *the only* seat at your table. I don't mean pushing everyone else away and making it so you're the only voice that can speak into your life.

In fact, that's an important principle: You should never sit alone at the table of your life. You need others to help manage your table well.

I remember those early days after I left Ramsey Solutions. For the first time in my life, I was on my own. No boss. No coworkers. No organizational mission statement or vision statement to memorize. It was just me, and I started out by trying to do everything myself.

For example, I knew I wanted to continue making impactful content on YouTube and turn it into a business. In the beginning, I wrote all the scripts myself. I did all the filming myself. I did all the video editing myself. I spent hours researching

Tables are
meant for
people, plural, to
come together
and connect.

algorithms and marketing keywords and all that. Whatever needed to be done to keep that content flowing, I was the one to make it happen.

It was exhausting. And I could tell the end product wasn't great.

Then I remembered my brother-in-law, Glen Henry, who has been killing it on YouTube for a long time. He'd grown his channel from zero to a million subscribers, and here I was plowing away trying to figure everything out on my own.

So I called him. Even from that first conversation, he provided insight on issues and ideas I didn't even know I was supposed to think about. It was Glen who showed me why I needed to hire a full-time video producer to help my content creation business.

"If you're trying to record *and* edit *and* host," he told me, "you're going to run out of juice. If you're going to build a scalable business around YouTube, you need to hire someone who can do the things you don't like doing so you can focus on doing what you love. All that extra stuff will take away from your creativity."

He was right. And he's been right on lots of similar issues. For that reason, Glen is one of the people I bring to my table as I continue to build my businesses as a thought leader. He has skills, expertise, and experience that can help me, so I make him a part of the table.

That's what I mean when I say your table includes your people.

When I visualize my own table, for example, I think of a long wooden table with ten or twelve comfortable chairs spaced around the outside. I'm seated at the head of the table, of course. Then, at the opposite end of the table is an empty chair. That one is reserved for Mrs. O'Neal. When I get married, my wife will take an equal seat at the head of my table so we can manage our lives together.

What about the other ten seats? They are filled with people I have intentionally invited to my table because they understand my mission and can help maximize my resources as I carry out that assignment.

Here are some of the people who sit at my table:

- The seat at my right is filled by my pastor, who is both my spiritual covering and one of my closest friends. He is the one person in my world who will always tell me the truth.
- The seat at my left is for my business mentor. I keep him close because I'm currently in the prime years of building my business, and I actively need his advice and wisdom in this moment.
- Another seat is shared by my therapist and emotional coach. They help me maintain my mental health, which is critical.
- Another seat is for my physical trainer, who helps me maintain my physical health. (My doctors also swap in and out of that seat when I need them.)
- Another seat is filled by my financial advisor so I can steward my wealth in a way that provides not only for my future but also for my family's future.
- Another seat is reserved for the team members at my company. Each of those people was specifically selected to help

build my table (and for me to help build theirs), so I make sure to give them a seat.

- Another seat is reserved for the people in my extended community who engage my content in different ways. People like you, reading this book right now. My community is made up of the people I aim to serve each day, so they get a seat at my table.
- Finally, I leave some open chairs at my table so different people with different expertise can rotate in and out as needed. (We'll talk more about maintaining a flexible table in chapter 9.)

See how it works? Your table is your life, and you've been given that table because you have an assignment to achieve—a purpose to fulfill. That assignment is too big to accomplish on your own, so you need to gather other people around your table who can help maximize your resources and make a real difference in your community.

That's the opportunity in front of you right now. When you manage your table well, you will enjoy the incredible blessings of abundance, wellness, and freedom. Just as important, you will play a huge role in helping others enjoy those blessings. You will make an impact on the lives of those you love most and on the lives of those you don't even know. You can literally change the world!

So pull out that chair. Take a seat at your table. Not just any seat though. *Your* seat. Right at the head.

Not sure what that means or how to make it happen? Just keep reading and find out.

CHAPTER 2

THE HEAD OF
YOUR TABLE

We've already talked about several tables, but I'd like you to imagine at least one more. This time I want you to think of a medieval setting, or something medieval-inspired like *Game of Thrones*.

Imagine walking through massive doors into a massive hall. The room is wide and spacious with tall pillars running the length of both sides. In the middle of that room is an enormous table. It's actually several enormous tables arranged end to end. The whole thing stretches like fifty feet long. That's the first thing you notice in the room: the table.

The second thing you notice is the people. Lots of people. Most of them are seated on long benches that ring the outside of the table, but a few ornate wooden chairs are also placed near the ends of the table on each side. There's another chair set up at the head of the table that really isn't a chair at all. More like a throne.

The third thing you notice after walking through those massive doors is the energy in the room. It's a nervous energy. A tension. Everyone is buzzing with conversation, but they're speaking quietly. People keep glancing at the huge doors you just walked through, then looking back to their companions. They seemed disappointed to see you when you walked in. Clearly they're waiting for someone else.

The rest of the hall is thick with that same tension. Musicians have gathered in one corner, and they're playing soft background music. Servants are standing all around the edges of the room. Some are holding trays of cups or pitchers of drink; others are keeping watchful eyes on people sitting around the table. Like the guests, most of the servants keep glancing at the doors behind you.

You take a moment to look back at the table, and you notice it's packed with food. Huge platters are spaced evenly around the board with just about every delicious delicacy imaginable—piles of steaks and chops, whole roasted chickens, little mountains of potatoes, colorful fruits, stacks of vegetables, and baskets of bread. Oh, and cakes. Huge cakes and sweet rolls and candies.

This is a feast! Yet, strangely, nobody's eating. Everybody has a plate in front of them, but the plates are all empty. The platters are untouched.

What's going on?

You're about to ask that question when the answer comes in the form of a long, loud trumpet blast. Instantly, the chatter around the table stops. The musicians playing their medieval version of elevator music hold their instruments at their sides. The whole room goes silent.

Then a man walks through the entry doors of the hall. If his confident stride and rich robes don't fill you in on his identity, the crown sure does. The king has arrived. He makes his way to the head of the table and stands for a moment in front of the throne-like chair. All the other guests rise. Still nobody speaks, but anticipation is building in the room. An intense energy.

With great ceremony, the king sits down at the head of the table. The guests wait a beat—maybe two seconds—and then return to their seats.

Just like that, the party gets started. I mean, it *really* gets started. The musicians start playing again, this time with volume. The servants scurry around the table pouring drinks, cutting food, and filling plates. People start talking and laughing and eating and enjoying themselves. One after another, each guest raises their cup toward the king in a salute of honor.

Okay, you're probably wondering why I'm imagining this medieval stuff. *What do kings and servants and all that nonsense have to do with my life, Anthony?*

Good question. The answer is that I wanted to show you a picture of what it means for someone to sit at the head of their table. Specifically, for *you* to sit at the head of *your* table.

That really is how things worked in medieval times. Whenever a king or a lord or someone important (meaning someone with money) sponsored a feast, all the guests gathered around the table with anticipation. But nobody started enjoying that feast until the king or queen or wealthy person officially kicked things off by taking their seat. That ceremonial act of sitting at the head of the table was like pushing the ignition button on a new car—it got everything started.

Here are some more examples. If you're a *Star Trek* fan, think of Captain Kirk or Captain Picard walking onto the bridge and sitting in the command chair. If you're into politics, think of the president walking into the Oval Office for the first time and taking a seat at the Resolute desk.

What we're talking about is a leader claiming the seat of

command. Sitting at the head of a table is an act of authority—of control.

Here's the principle I want to explore in this chapter: Every single person alive today is meant to sit at the head of their table. Every single person currently breathing and blinking was designed to assume command of that special place in their own unique lives.

Now here's the problem: Most of us aren't doing it. Most of us don't sit at the heads of our own tables, and we as both individuals and communities are experiencing the consequences.

What It Means to Be at the Head

Okay, let's get practical. What does it mean for you to sit at the head of your table? What does that actually look like in terms of everyday stuff?

First, remember that your table is your life. More specifically, your table is the huge collection of resources your Creator has given you to steward over the course of your life. As such, your table includes your physical body and physical health, your mental health, your time, your financial resources, your relationships, and so on. It also includes your spiritual health and your purpose—your God-given assignment.

That's your table.

To take your place at the head of your table, then, is to exercise authority over those resources. It means taking control of your life.

Think about your time as an example. Each of us is given the same amount of time each and every day. If you haven't done the

Every single
person alive
today is meant
to sit at the
head of their
table.

math, we all have 1,440 minutes from 6 a.m. Monday to 6 a.m. Tuesday. The same is true for Tuesday, Wednesday, Thursday, Friday, Saturday, and Sunday—we're given 1,440 minutes in each of those days, which is also 86,400 seconds each day.

So let me ask a real honest question: Do you have control over that time? If you think of those minutes as a form of currency—which they are—are you the one who decides how to spend them? Or have you given that authority to someone else? (Or even to several someones?)

I remember when I was getting ready to preach my first sermon as a minister. That was a big moment in my life. A big deal. I knew where I'd come from in terms of spiritual immaturity, and I knew the different obstacles I'd overcome to even reach that point in my life. I was so excited as the days ticked by and that moment drew closer and closer.

Then I got some tough news: My Cali dad couldn't come hear me preach. That may sound minor to you, and I know it is—at least, I know that intellectually. But my Cali dad was my first preacher. He's the first preacher I remember listening to when I was young. So the idea of standing behind a pulpit and delivering my first sermon without him in the room to hear me and support me . . . It was a rough loss.

Why couldn't Dad come? Because his job had a strict system for requesting time off. All the employees had to put in their requests for paid leave a year in advance, and those requests were granted based on seniority. My dad put in a request as soon as he heard I would be preaching on a particular Wednesday, but his request was denied.

Actually, that happened a few times. Dad wasn't able to

attend the launch party for my first book, *Debt-Free Degree*. He wasn't able to come celebrate with my former fiancée and me when we got engaged.

It's not like Dad didn't want to come to those important moments. He was as frustrated as I was. But at that point in his life, he wasn't fully in charge of how he spent his time. He didn't have the freedom to do what he wanted to do.

He wasn't sitting at the head of his table.

Maybe you're thinking, *Anthony, I work for a company. I have a boss. Does that mean I'm not sitting at the head of my table?*

Honestly, it might. Not because you have a job or a boss or a commute or anything like that. A person can sit at the head of their table and still work a nine-to-five. But if your boss or your job or your commute or anything else has such a large amount of control over your life that you are unable to be the person you are called to be—or if any of these influences make it impossible to move your life in the direction you know you should—then yes, it's likely you are not sitting at the head of your table.

This is about more than time, of course. Do you have control over your money and financial resources, or do other people have a significant claim on every dollar you make? Bankers. Creditors. Loan officers. Landlords. Do you have the freedom to invest your money in ways that contribute to your assignment? Or is that money already spent before you earn it? Grocery bills. Tuition. Memberships. Dating. Traveling.

Again, the issue here is control. Everybody has bills to pay. Lots of people have bosses. I want to be clear that paying bills or working for a company does not automatically mean you've been pushed aside from the head of your table. But if your creditors or your bosses have so much control over your life that you are unable to pursue your calling, then it's probably time to make a change.

What about wellness? Are you actively making decisions to manage your physical health? Mental health? Spiritual health? Are you able to invest in the relationships that are most meaningful to you?

In other words, do you have the freedom to manage and nurture the most important parts of your life? Or are you stuck working on a bunch of trivial problems each day that don't really matter to you?

Remember, you're the steward of your life. You've been given your table for a specific reason—a specific assignment. So if you're not able to carry out that assignment because other people or other organizations are pulling the strings, then something is wrong. You're not sitting at the head of your table.

Fortunately, that can change.

Who's at the Head of Your Table?

As a Black man, I'm happy to see the progress that's been made by the Black community in recent decades, and especially in recent years. Yes, there have been some bumps in the road lately, and a lot of problems still need to be solved. Even so, I'm grateful that our society is stepping forward toward equal opportunities for everyone.

THE HEAD OF YOUR TABLE

But there's one more big step I think the Black community needs to take: ownership.

If you look at our culture today, it becomes pretty clear that Black folks are some of the most creative people in the world. We see it in music. We see it in dance. We see it in sports. But often, Black people don't own their creativity.

The NFL is a great example. So many of the biggest stars are Black. A huge percentage of the players on any given team are Black. Yet not one of the team owners is Black.

Yeah, it's true that Black athletes in the NFL make millions of dollars over the course of their careers, which is great. Some of them even make tens of millions. But those who own the teams are making billions. And when those owners gather to make decisions and set their vision for the future of the league, Black folks aren't sitting at that table.

Until that moment arrives—until Black people fully take ownership of their tables and their place in American culture— we won't truly have freedom.

I was encouraged recently when Magic Johnson was part of the group that purchased the Washington Commanders. *Finally!* I thought. *A Black man owns an NFL team.* Then I realized Magic is just a minority partner (which is kind of an ironic way to phrase his involvement, I guess). He holds a very small portion of the team.

Progress, yes. But still a long way to go before Black people get a seat at that particular table.

What about *your* table? The biggest question you need to explore at this point in our journey together is this: Who is sitting at the head of your table? Someone is there. Someone is guiding and directing your life. And if that someone is not you, you've got a problem.

Here are some additional questions that can help you evaluate your situation:

- Do you have freedom to spend most of *your time* in ways that contribute to your assignment—to help fulfill your purpose? (If not, which people have the biggest influence in how you spend your time?)
- Are you free to spend the majority of *your financial resources* in ways that contribute to your assignment? (If not, which people determine where your money goes?)
- In a typical week, how many times do you make specific plans or specific decisions designed to benefit *your physical health*?
- In a typical week, how many times do you make specific plans or specific decisions to invest in *your mental health*?
- Are you the biggest source of direction when it comes to *your dreams and goals* for the future? (If not, who is?)
- Do *your closest relationships* help build and maximize your table, or do those relationships drain your resources?

I can't determine from afar whether you're sitting at the head of your table. But as I mentioned earlier, my experience tells me most people are not. Most people have been pushed to the sidelines of their own lives.

If that's why you picked up this book, don't give up. There's hope!

How to Sit at the Head

Ready for some bad news? Sitting at the head of your table is not like pulling out a chair in your dining room and taking a seat. It's not an instant decision or even a quick action. It does take some time and some intention. There's work involved, and some of that work may be uncomfortable.

Now for the good news: You can absolutely do it. Right now, in this moment, you have everything you need to start the process of taking your rightful place at the head of your table—at the head of your life.

You really just have three steps to take, and together, we're going to briefly walk through each one over the next few pages.

STEP 1: REMOVE ANYONE WHO DOESN'T BELONG

Yes, this is the uncomfortable part. But it's necessary. Why? Because you cannot take a seat at the head of your table if someone else is already sitting there.

Think of the work you just put in a few moments ago. Think of the list of questions you just answered. Then get really honest: Is someone else sitting at the head of your table? Or are *multiple* people competing for control of your time, your talents, your relationships, and your other resources?

Your answer could be a parent, for example. It's a sad reality that parents often assert themselves as the primary authority in their children's lives. Most of the time this happens out of a desire to help or to steer the child away from mistakes. "I'm just trying to help you see what's best for you right now," they may say. Or "I know what's best for my child."

You cannot take a seat at the head of your table if someone else is already sitting there.

THE HEAD OF YOUR TABLE

But *wanting* to help isn't the same thing as actually helping. And if parents sit at the head of their adult children's tables, they aren't helping; they're harming.

I once had a college student call in to my show live. Straight-A kid. Top of his class. He was still an undergrad, but his whole education was already planned out: earn a bachelor of science, attend medical school, find a specialty, find the right residency, and then live the rest of his life as a doctor. None of this was his idea. His mom made those choices for him long before he even started applying to colleges.

When this young man started listening to my show, he realized he didn't have a passion for medicine. Being a doctor didn't match what he knew about his assignment. Instead, he felt excited about a career in technology. After some research, he realized he could make good money right out of college in the tech field doing what he loved to do. Not only that, but he found a job he could do while he finished his undergraduate degree.

That's why he called my show, because he had just been through that conversation with his parents. At first his mom was upset—no surprise. But he had planned out what he would say. "Mom, I've already got a job. I'm getting paid now, and I'm guaranteed to make $85,000 a year as soon as I graduate."

Eventually, they understood. They even celebrated with him.

Think about that for a moment. This young man spared himself years of education he didn't want. He saved himself hundreds of thousands of dollars in school loans he and his parents couldn't afford. And he avoided years—maybe even decades—of going down a career path and assuming a plan for his life that didn't match his giftings and his purpose.

All because he decided to remove his mom from the head of his table and take his rightful seat.

There are plenty of other people who may be sitting at the head of your table: your spouse, your boss, your friends, your creditors, and so on. You may even be allowing the culture around you (or social media influences) to dictate how you manage your life.

No matter who is sitting in your space, you need to clear them out if you want a life of abundance, wellness, and freedom.

Sometimes that means a total separation—removing that person from your life altogether, especially if the relationship is toxic. That may sound harsh, but people who look to control the lives of others rarely let go just because they are asked nicely. Depending on the circumstances, it may also be possible to remove that person for a temporary period of time and then give them a chance to gradually reconnect.

Other times, removing someone from the head of your table means simply sliding them down to a more appropriate spot. For example, your boss should definitely have a seat at your table. They should have a role in helping you maximize your table, just as you have a role in contributing to your company. But your boss should never sit at the head of your table. They should not control your time or limit your ability to follow your God-given purpose.

How do you move a person from the head to a more appropriate place at your table? By setting boundaries. For example, you could say, "I am comfortable with this, but I am not comfortable with that." Or "I am willing to take these steps, but I am not willing to take those steps." Or "I respect your authority and guidance in this area of my life, but your authority does not extend to that area of my life."

Boundaries are a wonderful expression of freedom. And boundaries are one of the primary ways you can assert your authority as the head of your table.

STEP 2: ASSESS YOUR RESOURCES

Once you've made space for yourself at the head of your table, the next step is to assess your table—meaning, to spend time evaluating the resources that make up your table. What do you have to work with?

There's an old saying in the business world that goes, "You can't manage what you don't measure." That's true for your table, and it's also true for your role as a steward: It's hard to steward what you don't measure. Why? Because you need a sense of your available resources before you can determine the best way to apply those resources toward your assignment.

So take out a tape measure (metaphorically speaking) and take stock of your table. Maybe even write some things down:

- How well are you managing your time? Do you have enough margin to accomplish what you're called to accomplish, or do you need to free up some hours during the week?
- Describe your financial outlook right now. What are your assets? What are your debts?
- What's working well in your spiritual life?
- On a scale of one (poor) to ten (amazing), how would

you rate your physical health? What's working, and what's not working?

- On the same scale, how would you rate your mental health?
- How does your work situation match up with what you know about your God-given assignment? Are you being granted opportunities to fulfill your purpose?
- Which of your closest friends and family members are most valuable in terms of your assignment? Which ones are helping you move toward your goals?

I'm not asking you to get too detailed here. We're going to look more deeply at these elements of your table in later chapters. But I do think it's helpful to take an overall assessment of the resources currently included in your table.

STEP 3: INVITE OTHERS WHO CAN HELP

It's also helpful to take a quick look at the resources currently *around* your table. Remember, it's never good to sit at your table alone. You need other people to help maximize your life and nudge you forward in terms of your assignment.

As such, part of sitting at the head of your table is gathering the right people to join you, then inviting them to do so at the right times and in the right ways.

I recommend you start by looking for gaps. These are the basic categories of resources that make up your table:

- Your spiritual life
- Your mental health

- Your physical health
- Your work or career
- Your finances
- Your relationships

Which of those resources are you mostly trying to handle by yourself? To say it another way, in which of those areas do you not really have help? Those are gaps. And when you notice gaps, I strongly recommend you find people who can join you around your table and help manage those resources effectively.

But Anthony, who do I invite? How do I find the right people?

Great questions. Something that helps me is to spend a little time on the front end writing down what I'm looking for before I start searching for someone to join me at my table.

It may sound strange, but this book is a good example. I'm an author, but I'm not a writer. I've got a lot of ideas, and I'm constantly working out systems and strategies in my head. I love the process of workshopping those ideas and brainstorming new solutions with my team members.

But sitting down for hours and hours to type away at a laptop? Nope. No way. Not me.

So when I decided to write this book, I spent an afternoon thinking through what I would need most if I asked someone to join me at my table for a season. Here's the basic list I came up with:

- I wanted someone with experience working on *New York Times* bestsellers. I wanted a quality writer to help me.

- I wanted someone who had experience working with Black voices.
- I needed someone who could work relatively quickly and meet my deadlines.
- I really wanted to find someone I connected with on a personal level—someone who "got" me and could relate to me.

Once I had my list, the search itself was relatively easy. I just kept seeking options until I found someone who matched each of my criteria. (The fact that I found someone who shares my last name was just a bonus!)

You can follow the same approach as you look for people to join you at your table. Figure out your gaps. Get some clarity on what specific qualities you want or need in the people who might fill those gaps. Then, go out and search. Make connections. Be open and honest about what you're looking for and why it's important. When you find someone who matches your needs, you don't have to guess or hope things will work out. You'll know.

Like I said before, leaving Ramsey Solutions was one of the most difficult seasons of my life. In that moment I experienced a lot of anxiety about the future. This was my first time out on my own, and even though I knew I was making the right choice in terms of sitting at the head of my own table, I still felt terrified at first—and that terror only increased when I started hiring team members who would be counting on me.

It was scary!

It was also exhilarating.

I remember the moment when I knew I'd made the right choice. I'd been on my own for about a year, and I decided to do something that seemed radical—maybe even a little crazy. I took off July. Like, the whole month. From June 30 to August 1, I didn't create a single piece of content. I didn't write any reports or track down any contracts or seek out any networking connections.

Instead, I spent all of July pouring into myself. I gave myself a chance to breathe. To really rest, probably for the first time in years. I took time to think about the future—my dreams and visions and goals. I made a point of contemplating who I was created to be and what I was created to achieve.

I'm not gonna lie: It was awesome! It was wholesome. It was abundance, wellness, and freedom.

And if you're ready to see those same blessings in your life, let's start digging into the specific parts of your life that make up your table.

CHAPTER 3

SPIRITUAL WELLNESS

I t was time for me to leave Nashville.

I didn't want to—not really. I'd lived there for several years. Bought a home. Made friends. The city itself was booming, with lots of opportunities for business and real estate and networking. Not to mention lots of places to find great food and hear some of the best live music around. Nashville is a kicking town!

Still, it was time to go. I had just concluded my working relationship with Ramsey Solutions, and I was excited to start something new. But I understood it would be hard to focus on that "new" thing when so much of the "old" was still around. I needed a fresh start, which meant I needed a new place to inspire me.

After a lot of searching and thinking, I boiled everything down to three main options: Houston, Atlanta, and Charlotte, North Carolina. Honestly, I was leaning toward Charlotte.

That's when I got a call from my friend, Stephen Chandler. He's the senior pastor of Union Church outside of Baltimore, Maryland. A trusted mentor.

"What's up, AO?" he said when I picked up the phone. "Listen, I feel like I'm hearing from God about where you should move to, man."

That got my attention. By that time I'd known and respected Stephen for years, relying on him for advice and wisdom. In all that time, he had never said to me, "God is telling me you need to do this," or "God is telling me to talk with you about that." He had never used that type of language as my spiritual mentor.

Until now.

"I've been talking with Zai," he said, speaking about his wife. "We both think you need a community of your own. You need to be around people who love you. And you need accountability."

"Okay," I said. "So what does that have to do with me moving?"

"I think God is calling you here," he said. "To Maryland. I think He wants you to be a part of what we're building in this community."

Maryland? I'm a financial guy, so my first thoughts were mainly financial. That would mean moving from a place with no state income tax (Tennessee) to a place with a high state income tax. That would also mean moving from a city that was relatively inexpensive to a city that was very expensive. And moving from a familiar town to a new community that was completely unfamiliar.

Maryland? Really?

I told Stephen I would pray about it, and I followed through that same night. I spent at least an hour on my knees, asking God for wisdom and guidance about this decision. By the end of that time, I felt a strong sense of peace about moving to Maryland. I felt confident it was the right choice for me.

Looking back several years later, I *know* it was the right choice for me. I'm certain. I've thrived as a person, I've thrived in my business, and I've thrived in my faith as part of the Union Church family.

On my own, I never would have ended up where I am now—which is exactly why I'm so grateful to have someone like Stephen as a friend. I don't want to be on my own when it comes to my spiritual life. I don't want to rely only on my own faith or my own maturity or my own understanding of God's Word when it comes to something as important as my walk with God.

I need a spiritual partner. In my case, Stephen has been a mentor and friend. He is one of the only people in the entire world that I know will always tell me the truth even when I pretend I don't want to hear it.

You need that kind of person in your life as well. You need that kind of person at your table.

Speaking of which, it's easy to think about our tables in primarily tangible terms—things we can touch, like money. And possessions. And our bodies. And our jobs. And even our relationships. Lots of things included in your table are physical.

But that doesn't mean your table is *only* made of physical stuff, of touchable things. Far from it. A big part of your table is spiritual. As we'll see in this chapter, your table has a spiritual source. And maximizing your table means connecting it to spiritual power and spiritual people.

Your Table Has a Spiritual Source

I said in an earlier chapter that your table is your life, which is true. But I also want to make it clear that your table isn't about you. Not really. Making the most of your table isn't about making your life comfortable or enviable or more manageable.

That's because you are not the source of your table. Your

Creator is the source of your table. And He gave you that table—He gave you your life—for a specific purpose. For a spiritual purpose. You have a unique assignment in your community and in this world—one only you can accomplish.

So you are not the *source* of your table, but you are the *steward* of your table. You are called by God to use your table as a way of serving Him and blessing others. When that happens, you will also be blessed, which is important. But the cycle starts with God, not with you or me.

One of the most important themes in the Bible is that every human being was designed to have a relationship with God. We were created to connect with Him. When that connection is strong, we will have every opportunity to thrive. We will expand our tables and take hold of the abundance, wellness, and freedom God created us to enjoy. When that connection is not strong, however, we will have a difficult time managing our tables well.

That raises a big question: What does it mean to have a healthy relationship with God? What does that look like?

Personally, I like the word *alignment*. Having a healthy relationship with God means being aligned with God's plan for your life. God created you for a reason, for a specific purpose, which means you will experience the most joy and fulfillment when you live in a way that matches your purpose. But when your choices or your goals pull you away from that purpose, you won't be spiritually healthy. You won't have a meaningful life no matter what kind of salary or other outward sign of success you achieve.

So living in alignment with God is crucial to the success of your table. It's crucial to the success of your life.

You are not
the source
of your table.
Your Creator
is the source
of your table.

Will your life be perfect if you are in alignment with God? No. Living in alignment with God doesn't prevent you from experiencing things that are frightening, uncomfortable, or painful. We still go through difficult days and stressful seasons. But in my experience, being in alignment with God does make things better, even in the middle of those difficult days and stressful seasons. When I am aligned with God, I feel peace. I feel joy. I feel a true sense of accomplishment when I do something right. I feel supported and forgiven when I do something wrong.

It's weird to say, but when I'm in alignment with God, I can be walking through hell and still feel like everything's going to be okay.

That's not how I feel when I'm out of alignment.

Back when I was in middle school, I often walked home after my last class. On one afternoon in particular, I had to walk home in the middle of a storm. It was cold, so I was wearing a big jacket. But it was also rainy and very windy. I could hear the gusts howling around the different buildings and through the alleys as I trudged all the way home. It was not a fun walk.

There was one section of the route where I had to walk up this big, long hill. Seemed like it went on for several blocks, just going up, up, up. And because of the storm, the wind and the rain were pushing down, down, down. The wind especially caught against the folds of my jacket like a sail, and I felt like I was being physically pushed backward. Every step was a struggle. Every time I reached a street corner, I grabbed a light pole for support so I could rest a moment and catch my breath.

Honestly, about three-quarters of the way up that hill, I felt like giving up. I thought about just lying down and letting the wind blow me all the way back to school.

That's what life feels like when we're out of alignment with God. Every step is a struggle. Every inch of progress requires a mile's worth of effort. It's not just tough to manage your table in those conditions—it's just about impossible.

In fact, here's an important principle: You can't carry out your assignment in life when you're out of alignment with God.

Unfortunately, I know this from experience. I've survived a couple of seasons when I was out of alignment with God and did nothing to move forward with my assignment. One of those seasons came immediately after I finished high school.

Both sets of my parents kept a pretty strict home for me and my siblings. In California, we weren't allowed to watch TV during the week and were allowed only one hour on the weekends. My Carolina parents didn't allow me to listen to R and B, go to school dances, or attend many functions that conflicted with our church schedule. I grew up believing in God, and I wanted to do what I knew was right—but I was tired of feeling like I always had to say no to fun and my friends.

When I graduated high school, in my mind I also "graduated" from God. I said to the Creator of the universe, "Thanks but no thanks. I'm not rocking with You right now." My assignment at eighteen switched to becoming as popular as possible and getting as many ladies as possible. I poured all of my effort and all of my energy into achieving those two goals.

You know what? God let me achieve them. He gave me the desires of my heart. I became popular, I got lots of ladies, and everything seemed awesome for about six months.

Then life hit. Hard. All of a sudden I was homeless, I had no money, and I found myself in the back of my car trying to wash my body with Dawn dish soap before a date with a girl because I had no other place to go.

What happened? I had purposefully placed myself out of alignment with God. I chose to abuse my table by focusing only on myself—and God allowed me to experience the consequences.

In that moment—naked and trying to clean myself with dish soap because I still wanted to impress some girl—I realized how messed up my life had become. Right then, I stepped away from my rebellion and stepped back toward my heavenly Father. *God, if You allow me to return home*, I prayed, *if You will convince my father to let me back in the house, then I will never end up here again.*

Praise God, He did. And praise God, I haven't. Yeah, I've made some dumb decisions since then, and at times I've needed to adjust my life to realign with God. But I've never made a second choice to reject Him in that way.

If you've suffered through your own seasons of being out of alignment with God, you know it's no joke. It's serious. The only way to get back into alignment is to confess your mistakes and literally turn your life around. Get on your knees and apologize to your Creator. Say, "God, I stepped out, I admit it, and I am sorry." Ask Him to give you clarity on what He wants for your life—on what you need to do to get back in alignment with Him. Then get connected with spiritual people who can help you stay on the healthy path. (More on that in a moment.)

Your Table Requires Spiritual Power

Have you ever read a Bible verse that just knocked your socks off? It could be a Scripture passage you've heard a hundred times, but all of a sudden it surprises you in a big way.

That happened to me with John 15:5: "I am the vine; you are the branches. If you remain in me and I in you, you will bear much fruit; apart from me you can do nothing."

It was that last word that caught me: *nothing.*

When you read all of John 15, you'll see that Jesus was talking about alignment. When we are connected with Him and living in a way that is spiritually healthy, He says we will "bear much fruit"—meaning we will experience all the things we were designed to enjoy in our lives, including abundance, wellness, and freedom.

That makes sense. That feels right. But the second part of that verse feels like overkill. When we get out of alignment with God, I would have expected Jesus to say, "Apart from Me, you can do very little for My kingdom." Or maybe, "Apart from Me, you will be ineffective in your community."

But no. He said, "You can do nothing."

This is a big problem for us as human beings, and I think it's an especially big problem for us as Americans because most of us have been told we can do anything we put our minds to. Most of us are taught there are no limits to our success. Most of us have been promised the American Dream if we just work hard and make good decisions.

In other words, most of us genuinely believe we can build a pretty good table if we just put in the work. But we're wrong.

I don't know about you, but I don't want to sit at a table made by people. I don't want a life that is planned by people and powered by people—especially when *I* am one of those people! Instead, I want to sit at the table God built for me. I want my life to be filled with divine purpose and spiritual power.

For that to happen, I have to stop trying to make everything happen in my own strength.

Think of it this way: If I'm building something out of wood—maybe a table, for example—I could use a screwdriver to hammer in some nails. I could find one of those big, long, heavy screwdrivers with a metal handle. I could grab it by the pointy end and whack the nails with the handle. *Bam! Bam! Bam! Bam!* It would take me a long time, but eventually I could get those nails hammered down pretty close to where they need to be.

But would that be good management of my resources? No. Because a screwdriver is not designed to hammer things. I would be taking something designed for one purpose and misusing it by forcing it to accomplish a totally different purpose. Which means the job would take a lot longer and wouldn't be completed at a high level of quality.

Not only that, but if I kept using my screwdriver to hammer in a bunch of nails, it wouldn't be too long before that screwdriver broke. Maybe the handle would crack, or maybe the shaft would get bent at a weird angle. Then, when it came time for me to drive some screws into the wood, I wouldn't have the right tool to accomplish that task either. The whole system gets messed up when we don't use our tools the way they were designed to be used.

The same thing is true for the system God set up in our

I want to sit
at the table
God built for
me. I want my
life to be filled
with divine
purpose and
spiritual power.

communities, in our culture, and throughout the world. Our Creator designed you and me for a specific function—for a specific purpose. Just like a hammer is designed to hammer nails, you and I were designed to accomplish important things.

This is our assignment in life—our purpose or calling—and God gives us our table so we can carry out that assignment well.

The problem comes when we decide our assignment isn't good enough or that we're going to set it aside for a while to pursue something that feels more exciting to us—kind of like a screwdriver setting aside its design to hammer nails. Remember, God gave us our tables to equip us for carrying out *His* assignments for our lives. So when we use those resources to pursue our own purposes, we are misappropriating His gifts and messing up His plans.

Sometimes we even become proud about pursuing our own purposes. Sometimes we even brag to God! "Hey, God, look at everything I'm accomplishing here! Look at all this stuff I've done! Isn't it cool how much I'm contributing to Your kingdom?"

Jesus just shakes His head and reminds us of what He's already told us: "Apart from me, you can do nothing."

Here's my point: Your table is your life, and your life was given to you by God for a spiritual purpose. Therefore, you will waste everything you've been given if you fail to fill your table with spiritual power.

Where do you get that power? The Holy Spirit, for starters. That's another truth Jesus told us in the Bible:

If you love me, keep my commands. And I will ask the Father, and he will give you another advocate to help you and be with you forever—the Spirit of truth. The world cannot accept him, because it neither sees him nor knows him. But you know him, for he lives with you and will be in you. (John 14:15–17)

Don't overlook that incredible promise: You can invite the Holy Spirit to be part of your table. In fact, you *must* invite the Spirit to be part of your table! I recommend you invite Him every day. Ask Him to inform your decisions and guide your steps. Believe the truth that He is present with you and will empower you to achieve your purpose.

Your Table Needs Spiritual People

Let's recap what we've covered so far. First, your table has a spiritual source. Your life comes from God and is designed by God. Second, because that's true, your table requires spiritual power. You can't make your life "go" on your own. You can't achieve anything meaningful on your own, let alone experience abundance, wellness, and freedom. You need spiritual power, which begins with inviting the Holy Spirit to your table.

Third, you also need to make room at your table for spiritual people. You need trusted individuals who can speak with you in an honest way about the spiritual nature of your life—the spiritual nature of your table.

Stephen Chandler is one of those people at my table. Another is Dr. Dharius Daniels, who has been an amazing mentor for several years now.

I remember when I was considering walking away from

Ramsey Solutions. As you can guess, many doubts filled my mind at the prospect of leaving such a rewarding and lucrative career. I faced a lot of uncertainty. In fact, I was so anxious about the decision in front of me that I hopped in my car and drove down to Atlanta to speak with Dharius. I needed his input for this critical choice.

Sitting in his office, I was honest about my biggest reservation. "PD, it's hard to walk away from this salary," I told him. "Six figures!"

He nodded. He was listening. But he wasn't convinced. "What you are making now in a year at that company," he told me, "I believe you can make in a month out on your own. The impact you make in a year now, you can also make in a month out on your own."

I was stunned. But still struggling. "How though?" I asked. "I'm having trouble seeing it, man."

He just smiled. "That's why I'm here. I have been called into your life to help you see spiritual things you can't see right now."

That is the first blessing we receive when we invite spiritually healthy people to sit at our tables: We gain access to women and men who are able to see things we cannot see. This is true for several reasons. Maybe we're blinded by our circumstances. Maybe we're obstructed by immaturity or anxiety or doubt. Maybe we can't see past our own fears. Whatever the reason, we need others around us who can offer important information because they bring different perspectives.

The second blessing we receive when we invite spiritual people to our tables is accountability. Remember what it says in Proverbs? "As iron sharpens iron, so one person sharpens another" (27:17).

After all, it's one thing to have dreams and goals and plans as an individual. But it's a whole different thing to have a team of people dedicated to helping you reach those dreams and goals and plans—a team that keeps you pointed in the right direction. I need people in my life who will tell me when I'm getting off track. "Anthony, I thought you said you were going to head in this direction for the next month. How's that going?" someone might ask. Or "Anthony, you told me you were going to pray every morning for a week before you made this decision. What did you hear from God during those prayers?"

Do you have those kinds of people in your life? At your table? If not, you need to invite them in.

Actually, that's an important step: the invitation. One time I was golfing with Stephen Chandler when we started discussing a bad decision I'd made a few months before. "Man, I knew that was going to blow up in your face," he said, chuckling.

"What?" I was shocked. "Why didn't you say anything?"

"Because you didn't ask!" He was still chuckling, but then his face got serious. "Anthony, I'm not going to inject myself into any part of your life where you have not invited me. That's not how accountability works."

I stood still for a full minute. Thinking. Processing. Then I looked him in the eyes and said, "Bro, I give you space and a place to be part of my life as an accountability partner—and I mean every part of my life. I am inviting you to speak up any time you see me moving in the wrong direction."

Have you done that with those closest to you? It starts with your spouse and family, of course. But also your close friends and mentors. You need to actively invite them to speak into your life and tell you the truth.

Now, here are two big questions: *How do I identify the right people to invite to my table? What does a "spiritual person" look like?*

I've mentioned my two primary spiritual mentors: Stephen Chandler and Dharius Daniels. Now, those two men just happen to be senior pastors, which I admit is pretty lucky for me. I feel very fortunate to have two men of such high caliber in my life—although, speaking frankly, senior pastors are always busy people, which means I do have to wait patiently sometimes to spend time with those men. Even so, I recognize I am blessed to have access to both Stephen and Dharius, and to know they love me as brothers.

I do want to make this clear though: Your spiritual mentor doesn't have to be a pastor, bishop, or minister of any kind. In fact, it's likely that the spiritual people at your table will not be pastors. There's just not that many to go around in each community.

Those you invite to your table may be good friends or cousins or coworkers or members of your small group. You have many options, but this is critical: The people you choose must be spiritually healthy. Meaning, they should love God and have a genuine relationship with Him. They should live the kind of life that produces real fruit for God's kingdom.

You might be wondering, *How do I know if someone is spiritually healthy?* Good question. The answer is to watch and listen. Watch what they do, listen to what they say, and then evaluate whether they are the type of person who will move you forward toward your spiritual goals. You want to avoid the type of person who will drag you down or push you back.

When you think about it, you could get a pretty good idea about a person's physical health by watching them for a day. You wouldn't know for certain—you wouldn't be able to tell exactly what was happening underneath their skin. But plenty of clues would provide evidence in one direction or another.

Man, that's his second pack of cigarettes today. He smokes like a chimney! Unhealthy. *Look at the way she's running around with those kids. She's got more energy than a Jack Russell terrier.* Healthy.

You can make similar evaluations when it comes to a person's spiritual life. The more time you spend with a person, the more you will be able to observe who they really are—what they value and what they genuinely believe. When you find someone who genuinely values God and believes in His plan for your life (His assignment), then you've found someone who can help you maximize your table and move forward with a spiritual perspective.

Let me finish with the same questions I asked earlier: Do you have those kinds of people in your life? At your table? Do you regularly engage with people who love God and are willing to help you love God? People who genuinely care for you and are willing to invest their time and energy into maximizing your table?

If so, I recommend you get down on your knees right now

and thank God for those people—for those gifts. Ask Him to help you bless them in the same way they are blessing you.

If not—if you're missing those people at your table right now—then I strongly recommend you get down on your knees and ask God to bring them to you. Then keep asking until they pull up a chair.

CHAPTER 4

MENTAL WELLNESS

I was on a date with a young lady one evening. We'd seen each other a couple of times, and I'll admit I was interested in learning more about her romantically. I'll be real: She was beautiful. In my eyes she was a great catch. She had a great career. Loved God. And it seemed like she thought those things were true about me as well.

There was hope in the air.

"Hey, you wanna get together on Friday night?" I asked her. "I'll be free once I finish with my therapist around four, so we could—"

"Therapist?" She cut me off like a knife. "Uh, should I be aware of something? What's wrong with you?"

I'd been looking down at the dessert menu, but the sharpness of her voice pulled my gaze back up to her face. Her eyes were narrow and suspicious. Her mouth was a thin, joyless line. Her arms were crossed over her chest.

She was staring at me like I was an illness she should run from.

"With me?" I asked, still trying to figure out how the situation had gone from flirty to frightening in four seconds. "What's wrong with *you*?" I shot back.

Let's just say there was a lot less hope in the air throughout the rest of the evening.

A lot of people are talking about mental health these days—specifically, how our culture struggles with mental health. Issues like anxiety and depression. Stress. Addictions of all kinds. Loneliness and isolation. Suicidal thoughts and actions. I hear the stories on the news or on podcasts. I read the statistics in articles and books.

Here are just a few of the numbers so you can see what I mean:

- More than 19 percent of adults in the United States dealt with an anxiety disorder in the past year.
- A little more than 8 percent of adults have experienced major depression. That's twenty-one million people.
- About 7 percent of US adults will experience post-traumatic stress disorder (PTSD) at some time in their lives.
- Suicide was the twelfth leading cause of death in the United States during the year 2020. It was the second leading cause of death for young people ages ten to fourteen and twenty-five to thirty-four.[1]

So yeah, people are struggling.

At the same time, it seems like a lot of people keep the concept of their own mental health at arm's length. We're aware of what's happening with society as a whole, and we know about others from our circles of family and friends who seem to be having trouble. But we don't think much about what's happening inside our own hearts and heads.

In fact, sometimes we try really hard to avoid thinking about it.

That's a problem for several reasons—one of the biggest being that your mental health is a hugely important part of your table.

In a Bad Place

For most of my life, I had no idea I was in a bad place with my mental health. Looking back, I can see I was carrying a lot of anxiety. Several times I went through seasons of depression. Like I shared earlier, I even spent a short period of time homeless and sleeping in my car.

But had you asked me how I was doing during those years, I would have said, "I'm fine." And I would have meant it. I genuinely believed I was just riding the regular ups and downs of life.

In the same way, if you had asked the people closest to me—my friends and family—how I was doing, they would have said, "He's great." And they would've meant it too. Aside from my parents, the people who knew me best had no idea I was living out of my car or how much I was struggling. (Which makes sense, because *I* had no idea how much I was struggling.)

One of the reasons for my poor mental health was a habit I'd developed of always putting other people ahead of me—and not in a good way. I wanted to please everyone. I wanted to be liked by everyone. So I started figuring out what people wanted me to say, then saying it. I figured out what people wanted me to believe, then believed it. I figured out what people wanted me to do, then did it.

This happened with my teachers and my friends growing up. It happened with my coworkers and my bosses when I entered

Your mental health is a hugely important part of your table.

the workforce. It even happened with my fellow pastors and church members when I entered the ministry.

Whatever situation I found myself in, I didn't think about what I wanted or needed. Instead, I thought about everyone else but me. *If I say this, what will they think? If I do this, how will that reflect on my company (or my church or my family)? If I don't do this, how will that group of people react?*

During those years, I was constantly reinforcing the negative belief that my thoughts and my feelings and my needs didn't matter. The way I lived communicated that, in my view of the world, everyone else was more important than me.

Eventually I started to dread being around other people. I lost the motivation to go to church. I started avoiding certain people in the office and in my community. I was mentally and emotionally exhausted, but nobody knew because I poured whatever energy I had left into putting on a good face and pretending everything was okay.

Things finally turned around when I met a girl. No, not the girl who wanted to know what was wrong with me, but another young lady who had caught my attention several years earlier. This girl was also attractive and interesting and self-confident. We went on several dates, and I thought things were going well.

Then she sat me down one evening at dinner and told it to me straight: "I think you're a good guy," she said, "but there's something wrong with you, and I can't move forward with you. You need to see a therapist."

Whoa! Talk about a wake-up call.

From the jump, I knew what she was telling me was right—that she was pointing to something I actually needed. So I asked her to help me. She hooked me up with her therapist and walked me through the stage of being "in therapy" for the first time.

After several sessions, I started to recognize that though thinking of others is important, thinking about myself is also important. Taking care of myself is important. Instead of letting everyone around me determine my beliefs and my actions, I needed to start thinking *of* myself and *for* myself. I wouldn't have used this language at the time, but I needed to be at the head of my table.

That's an important connection, because being pushed away from the head of one's own table is one reason why so many people struggle with mental health. When you're not sitting at the head, you're always at the mercy of others. You're always waiting for something to go wrong—for the other shoe to drop. That kind of stress can be a big source of anxiety and depression.

I remember one time when I was working at the collection agency in California, and I got a text from my boss: "I need to see you tomorrow morning."

My first thought was, *Oh no! What did I do? I'm about to be fired!* I showed the text to all my friends that evening and tried to get their opinion on what was going on. "What do you think he wants? Why would he want to see me?" I spent the whole night sweating under the sheets in my bed, trying to figure out what I'd done wrong and how I was going to pay my bills if I lost my job. I was miserable.

Of course, when I did check in with my boss the next morning, it was all good news. He actually wanted to congratulate me on the way I'd handled a particularly difficult account—he just wanted to do it face-to-face instead of through email. Walking out of his office, I felt relieved and stupid at the same time.

Why did I have such an extreme reaction to something as small and silly as a text message? Because I didn't have control or authority in my own life. I'd allowed myself to be pushed off to the side of my table, and it was stressing me out.

Thankfully, I didn't stay there. Because of therapy and my own growth as a person, I've learned to treasure my mental health as a vital part of my table. I want to make certain you can do the same, especially as we continue to explore what it means to manage your own table.

Your Number One Asset

Quick question: What's your most important asset?

If you're not familiar with financial terms, an *asset* is a resource you own that generates value of some kind. If you own a house, for example, that would be an asset. You have to pay for it, but even if you are working through a thirty-year mort-gage, that house will likely appreciate over time and generate more money—making it an asset.

So what about you? What's your most important asset? Meaning, what do you own or control that contributes the most overall value to your life?

Let me help you out with an answer here. Even though we likely haven't met, I would still be able to tell you that your mind is your most important asset. Your brain. Your ability to think and feel and process and understand. Everything you want to experience and accomplish in life is dependent on your mind functioning properly and giving you the tools to move forward.

Your number one asset is not your money. Your number one asset is not your spouse. It's not your home or your car or your 401(k) or anything else you can see or touch. Your number one asset is your mind.

I often share this principle with young entrepreneurs: Mind your business, because your mind is your business.

The reason I make such a big deal about mental health is because your mind determines the quality and caliber of your table. Whatever plans you have for maximizing your resources, maturing as a person, and making progress toward your specific assignment in life—it all starts with your mind. It all starts with your ability to think and dream and mentally navigate the complexities of life.

For that reason, you and I need to be good stewards of our minds. Managing our minds well is a critical part of managing our tables.

The first step in stewarding your mind is to make sure it has everything it needs, starting on a physical level. For example:

- Your diet impacts your mental health, so are you feeding your brain in a way that is healthy? Are you giving your mind the raw ingredients it needs to function well?
- Many studies show that people who are sleep-deprived function at a similar level to people who are drunk.[2] So are you giving your mind enough rest each night? In the long term, do your sleep habits help your brain or harm it?

Mind your
business,
because your
mind is your
business.

- "Mind-altering drugs" are given that name for a reason. Do you use substances such as drugs or alcohol that impact your mental health? Are you chemically dependent on "safe" drugs such as sugar or caffeine?
- Stress has a corrosive effect on both our bodies and our minds. Are you able to manage stress in a way that's healthy?

Beyond physical stuff, the second step for stewarding our minds is to be realistic about problems and deal with them as they arise. Again, it's been my experience that many people turn a blind eye to their own mental health. And even when they know something is wrong—even when the symptoms are so obvious and so frequent that they can't be ignored—many people still refuse to get help.

Why? Because there's a stigma attached to getting help for our mental health. Even in our modern, progressive, compassionate world, lots of people out there refuse to seek out that kind of help because they think it means something is wrong with them on the inside. They think it means they're broken. Or weird. Or weak.

There's a running joke in the Black community that we don't change the oil in our cars until the check-engine light on the dashboard turns on. There's more truth to that than I'd like to admit, but I don't think it's just a Black thing or a male thing or a Christian thing. It's a people thing.

But waiting to get help until the last possible moment isn't helping us. It's hurting us.

Earlier I said that stewarding our minds means dealing with

problems as they arise. Actually, though, the best way we can manage our mental health is to deal with problems *before* they arise. That means regularly evaluating ourselves and checking to see if any issues are starting to creep up—if any habits or patterns or ways of thinking are starting to become a problem.

That's where therapy comes in. Seeing a therapist isn't just for dealing with problems from the past. (Such as: "Tell me about your mother when you were a child.") No, therapy gives us a way to identify minor problems in the present so we can prevent them from becoming major issues in the future.

Think about the nicest car you can imagine. A brand-new Bentley, for example, right off the lot. Or a Porsche 911 Carrera. Or a Mercedes-Benz S-Class. Imagine opening the hood on one of those cars and looking down at the new engine. Every part gleaming. Every bolt tightened down to perfection, not a grease stain in sight. The whole package just humming and purring like a dream.

That's what your mind should be like. That's what your mind *can* be like—if you choose to steward it well.

A Listening Ear and a Truthful Tongue

You've probably noticed there isn't much therapy-type stuff in this chapter, and that's intentional. I'm not qualified to give out mental health advice because I'm not a therapist. I'm not a counselor.

Here's what I *am* qualified to say: Since mental health is part of your table, you need to gather some people around you who can help you manage that resource well. For me, that started with choosing to see my therapist on a regular basis—not only when there's a crisis and I'm desperate for help, and not only once a year for a checkup.

Personally, stewarding my mental health means seeing my therapist *at least* every month. It means making my mind a priority, not just in my personal life but also as part of my business—as part of my assignment in this world.

I also have a seat at my table for an emotional coach. There's another running joke that says men are aware of only three emotions: mad, sad, and glad. My coach helps me identify the broader range of what I'm feeling and especially helps me identify and process strong emotions I've experienced over a period of time. It's another helpful tool in the toolbox for my mental health.

I wish I had found these types of resources much earlier—and definitely before I became a pastor. Early on in my life, some ideas that weren't healthy were deeply ingrained in my mind. I looked at people and judged them wrongly because of those unhealthy ways of thinking, and the judgments caused some real problems I wish I could have avoided. Therapy would have helped me identify those issues long before they became a problem.

Enough about me. Who do you have at your table that can help you effectively steward your mental health? Who do you need to invite to your table to better manage the resource of your mind?

Obviously, I think everyone can benefit from therapy, so it's my opinion that most people should invite a therapist to their table if they don't already have one. Beyond that, I can think of two specific people (or maybe two types of people) who also need to be present at your table to help you maximize your resources and complete your assignment: You need a listening ear and a truthful tongue.

First, you need people at your table who will listen to you—and I mean *really* listen to what you have to say.

Have you ever been part of a conversation and then realized the people you are talking to aren't really listening? You can see their eyes glazing over. They're partly paying attention to what you're saying, but they seem to be using most of their brainpower to figure out what they're going to say as soon as you're done talking. Or they're listening to you mainly because this conversation gives them an opportunity to express their opinions.

Have you ever been around people like that?

Me too.

What you need at your table is someone who will actually listen to you. Someone who maintains eye contact and leans in when you're talking. Someone who asks questions because they want to understand you. Someone who is willing not only to be a sounding board but also to keep you accountable after the conversation. For example: "Hey, Anthony, you said you were going to call your mom this week and talk through some of those issues. Did you call her?"

You need a listening ear at your table.

Second, you need a truthful tongue. You need someone who, without a doubt, will tell you the truth when you need to hear it. Specifically, you need someone who will tell you the truth even when you don't ask for it—even when you don't want to hear it.

Several years ago I was working in an office with cubicles, and I had an associate who liked to have loud conversations on speakerphone during her lunch break. Usually I put in headphones to drown her out, but one day I couldn't find them. I did my best not to listen, but the discussion was interesting enough (and loud enough) to pull me in.

To make a very long story short, my associate was a single mom with a ten-year-old son. The dad had been out of the picture for many years, but he was trying to reconnect with his boy. The day before, he'd asked my associate for permission to take their son to a game.

"I told him no," my associate said. "After everything he did to me? No way." The father had apparently cheated on her, which is why the relationship ended.

There was silence for several moments on the other end of the line. Then the friend asked, "What did he say exactly? What did he ask?"

"He said he wanted to get more involved in his son's life. He said he wanted to take him to a basketball game. Can you believe the nerve?" My associate's voice was packed with pain and resentment. I could tell she was still hurt by what had happened even after all those years had gone by.

"And you said no." The friend's voice was calm but concerned. "Are you sure that's a good idea?"

"Of course! You remember exactly what he did to me, girl! He don't deserve a thing."

The friend was silent for another long stretch. Then she said, "Let me get this straight. You're going to deny him the chance to be a father because he was a bad boyfriend? Ten years ago?"

"I mean, basically," was the response.

"So when your son gets older and asks why his father isn't in the picture, are you going to tell him it's because you didn't want his dad in his life—because his dad hurt *you*?"

"I mean . . . he did hurt me though. You know that."

"Yeah, but he's trying not to hurt your son." The friend wasn't letting go. "He's trying to be a father."

"Girl!" My associate was getting upset now. "You're supposed to be on my side!"

"Uh, I *am* on your side," her friend answered. "I'm on the truth's side. I'm on your son's side. I know that man did you wrong back when you were dating. He was a jerk—100 percent. But he's trying to change. Now you know I love you and I'm here for you, but you are wrong."

Boom! Even in my own relatively immature state, I was impressed by this friend's maturity. She had empathy for my associate. She expressed love and support for my associate. And she straight-out told my associate she was wrong.

In other words, she told the truth.

We all need people like that in our lives—and at our tables. Remember what Jesus said: "Then you will know the truth, and the truth will set you free" (John 8:32).

CHAPTER 5

PHYSICAL WELLNESS

For more than thirty years of my life, people told me I was too skinny. Like, to my face. They just came out and said it. "You're too skinny, Anthony."

Growing up, my friends told me all the time. So did my parents. "Why don't you eat a little more, Anthony? You're too skinny."

When I started dating as a young adult, several ladies shot me down because of my lighter frame. Do you know how frustrating it is to work up your courage, dress up in your best outfit, turn your charisma up to the max as you approach a lady—and then hear her say, "Nah, nah. You too skinny"?

If that's never happened to you, I can tell you it's super frustrating!

I remember the day I decided enough was enough. I was finally making some decent money at a good job, so I bought myself some workout clothes and got me a gym membership. I was ready to put an end to my skinny problem once and for all.

For several weeks, I went to that gym every day, and I worked out hard. I'd never worked out before, and I didn't really have any idea of what I was doing—but I was serious about making some progress fast. So I found the heaviest weights I could handle, and I lifted them. I raised dumbbells over my head. I pushed bars up off my chest. I pressed weights with my legs. I pulled stuff up with my back.

Whatever I could do, I did it, and I did it as many times as I could. I was going to get pumped!

Pretty soon, I started experiencing pain in my muscles. Pain all over my body. *That's good*, I thought. *No pain, no gain. Keep going.* I kept going.

Then I started to experience *serious* pain in my muscles. And my joints. And even my bones. *No problem*, I told myself. *This much pain must mean I've got some serious muscles just around the corner. Keep going.* I kept going.

Then I started having trouble getting out of bed in the morning. My back was in agony. My arms were rubber. My legs felt like they were about to fall off.

Finally, it started to get through to my brain that maybe something was wrong. Maybe I needed to get this checked out. So I went to my doctor and told him all the symptoms I was experiencing.

"How long have you been lifting weights?" he asked me.

"Three weeks now." I couldn't quite keep the pride out of my answer. Almost a whole month!

"And are you sure you're lifting the right way?" he asked.

"Yes," I said. "I'm . . . Wait, what do you mean?"

"I mean, are you using the right technique? Are you lifting in a way that is safe for your body?"

Now I was feeling confused. Technique? Safe? "Uh, can you explain that?"

By now the doctor had a pretty good idea of what had happened to me. He shook his head. "You're walking around like a ninety-year-old man," he said. "That's not supposed to happen when you work out."

"It's not?"

He shook his head again. "No. You need to get a personal trainer and figure out how to lift weights the right way. Then you'll be able to build muscle mass without harming yourself."

"Oh." I was feeling a little deflated (no pun intended). A little embarrassed. "That's good to know."

He was right, of course. I connected with a personal trainer at my gym, and he talked with me for a long time about my goals—what I wanted to achieve in terms of my health and over-all strength, how much I wanted to work out in a week, and so on. Then he talked me through a workout plan, which included alternating different types of lifts on different days so I could give muscle groups time to rest and rebuild. Then he showed me the proper technique for the lifts he wanted me to start with at my level.

No surprise, his plan worked. I still brought the same level of energy and intensity to each session in the gym, but now that energy was invested in the right way—and it started paying dividends.

Goodbye, "too skinny"!

My point is that I needed help to manage my physical wellness—and I'm not the only one. We all need that kind of help. Why? Because our physical bodies and physical health have a huge impact on every other aspect of our lives.

Your Body and Your Table

Here's the main point I want to communicate in this chapter: When we do a good job of stewarding our bodies and our physical health as part of our tables, we will put ourselves in a great position to fulfill our God-given assignments over the course of our lives. Why is that true? Because when we are physically well, we have the energy necessary to work hard at our goals, we have the strength to push through obstacles, and we are statistically much more likely to live longer—which means we'll have more time to achieve more.

Now, I know that's not rocket science. It's a pretty basic truth that when we take care of our physical health, we will typically feel better and live longer. No surprise there.

The problem is, most of us know the importance of taking care of our physical health when it comes to *information*, but we're not so diligent when it comes to *application*. Look at these statistics to see what I mean:

- More than 40 percent of adults in the United States are obese according to the National Institutes of Health.[1]
- Almost 20 percent of children are obese. That's one child out of every five![2]
- The Centers for Disease Control estimates that twenty-eight million people in America are cigarette smokers. (That's almost 12 percent of adults.)[3]
- More than 10 percent of US citizens over the age of twelve (!) are addicted to alcohol, and more than 140,000 Americans die every year from the effects of alcohol.
- Almost forty million Americans are living with diabetes.[4]
- Roughly one-third of Americans don't get enough sleep at night. In fact, things are so bad that almost 40 percent

of adults report falling asleep without meaning to during the day.[5]

I could go on, but you get the point. A pretty big number of Americans are in rough shape physically. We are not a healthy nation, and things seem to be getting worse instead of better. That's bad news when it comes to stewarding our tables, mainly because our physical bodies are crucial to our well-being.

Your physical wellness is one of the most important resources you've been given to steward as you carry out your God-given assignment. You might think of your body as the legs on your table: It supports the other important elements of your life and gives them the strength to stand. But when your physical health is in bad shape, the whole table is in danger of collapsing.

Thankfully, the opposite is true as well. When your physical health is well maintained, you drastically increase the opportunities for your entire table to thrive.

My first year at Ramsey Solutions, I got myself into an awesome routine. At the gym by five every morning. Finished my workout at six. A quick shower, a little breakfast, and I was sitting at my desk in my office by seven thirty, ready to tackle the day. It was a good feeling.

You know what I noticed during those years as I maintained that routine? That good feeling stayed with me throughout the day. I had consistent, long-lasting energy. I was focused and sharp. I felt dialed in and confident—at the top of my game.

Then, after I went out on my own, I was so concerned about making my new business a success that I dropped my old routine. I still worked out sometimes, but not every day. Actually,

I'll be honest: That first year on my own, I didn't work out most days. I was so anxious to be successful that I wanted to get started with my new projects as early as possible. I let my workout routine slip to the back of my mind.

You know what I noticed after several months of ignoring my physical health? I no longer felt dialed in each afternoon. Honestly, when two o'clock rolled around, I felt tapped out. My brain got all fuzzy and my head got heavy. I had to start taking naps so I could push through and stay awake into the evening.

What was happening? I'd stopped taking care of my health, so my health stopped taking care of me. It's that simple.

The same principle is true for you. When you take steps to maintain your physical health and do a good job of managing your body, you'll feel better. When you feel better, you'll do better. And when you do better, you'll fulfill your God-given assignment in ways that impact your life and your family and your community for generations to come.

It really is that simple.

Your Body and Your Enemy

I know I've mentioned it several times already, but this is the kind of truth that's worth repeating: Your table is a gift from your Creator. Each and every resource you manage in your life—including your body, your mind, your money, your relationships, and much more—is a gift offered to you by God. Those gifts are His way of equipping you to carry out your assignment in this world.

You are a steward of your table.

It's also important for me to point out that God isn't the only spiritual power out there interested in your table—in your life. You have an enemy. His name is Satan, and he is real. His demons are real. And they have a real interest in smashing your table to bits.

I know many people (and even some entire faith traditions) find it silly to believe in Satan. Some preachers and denominations think of the devil as a metaphor for the problems of the world, not as a real being who really exists. I'm going to speak frankly on this: They're wrong. And all you have to do to see that they're wrong is turn on the news and watch all the ways chaos and corruption are erupting in our world.

Metaphors don't create the kind of mess we see in our world. Evil does that.

The Bible says Satan's goal is "to steal and kill and destroy" (John 10:10). It describes the devil as "a roaring lion looking for someone to devour" (1 Peter 5:8).

That's the way Satan feels about you. He's not interested in making your life less convenient. He's not trying to make you feel sad. He doesn't want to give you a bad name or block your promotion or keep you from going to church by tempting you with a football game.

No, the devil is out to devour your table. He uses his demons to steal, kill, and destroy anything that helps you experience abundance, wealth, and freedom. Satan wants to grind your face into the dust.

Maybe you're wondering, *Anthony, what does all this have to do with my physical wellness?* Good question.

The answer is that your table is only as strong as its weakest

Metaphors don't
create the kind
of mess we see
in our world.
Evil does that.

point. Which means if Satan wants to destroy that table (which he does), he doesn't have to attack it holistically. He doesn't have to attack your entire life—your physical body, your mental health, your finances, your relationships, your career, *and* your spiritual life. He doesn't have to mess with it all at the same time. Instead, he just needs to find one weak spot. He just needs one area where you've let your guard down.

For many of us in America today, our weak spots are our physical and mental health. Sometimes one or the other, and sometimes both. We've already addressed the importance of always minding your business because your mind is your business (chapter 4), so I'm not going to repeat those ideas here.

But I do want to focus on two specific ways Satan is seeking to attack our tables by attacking our physical health.

SATAN WANTS TO LIMIT YOUR EFFECTIVENESS

First, by corroding your physical health, the devil wants to erode your effectiveness at fulfilling your God-given assignment. As I mentioned earlier in this chapter, there's a strong relationship between how healthy we are and how much we can accomplish. When we do a poor job of stewarding our bodies, we're often unable to accomplish what we'd like, even when it comes to important assignments.

Sometimes our lack of physical health can create a distraction. It can move our focus away from what's most important because we're stuck thinking about our bodies.

I've experienced both sides of that coin. For example, one time I was scheduled to speak at a huge conference in one of those big sports arenas. There were about twenty thousand people in the audience. Loud music and huge video screens— the works. The whole environment was jumping.

Back in the greenroom before going onstage, I stopped to look at myself in the mirror. My honest thought was, *I look good*. And I did! This was during a season of my life when I was working out consistently. I had worked out that very morning, in fact, and I was in great shape. My clothes were popping. My hair line was crispy. Even my shoes were gleaming.

I walked out on that stage with confidence. With swagger. Which means I wasn't distracted by my physical appearance. *Is my stomach pooching out too much? Am I in danger of a belch slipping out while I talk?* I wasn't worried about anything as I spoke that day. Instead, I was able to fully concentrate on my assignment of informing and inspiring the audience to help improve their lives. I was zoned in on my mission.

Other times, though, my lack of physical health has been a distraction from my mission. There have been a few times onstage when I realized I was sucking in my stomach because I didn't want people to think I was overweight. I was supposed to be speaking and helping people with their lives, but I could barely breathe from trying to hold in my gut! I wasn't as effective as I could have been because of a simple, small distraction.

Those little distractions can happen all the time. Like when we don't eat the right kinds of food, our bodies make us pay the price, don't they? We have to deal with gases and gurgles throughout the afternoon. Or heartburn. Or worse. Those may seem like minor issues, and they are in the grand scheme of things. But on any given day, they can keep us from performing at our best.

Other times our lack of physical health is a major issue. A major problem.

For example, have you met people who just seem to have no energy? It takes everything they have to get through the day. They get up, they go to work, they watch TV, and they go back to bed. That's it. Or have you met older folks who seem to have lost their strength and passion in their later years? The idea of retirement can become more than just a lifestyle. It can become a mentality in which we think, *We have made our contribution, so now we're finished. We're out of the race.*

But that's not how God planned to use those later years. He wants us to steward our tables in every season of life because He has an assignment that applies to each one. He has work for us to do at every age—which is why we need to make the effort to maintain our health and keep our bodies strong.

Major medical issues are another way Satan can use our lack of physical wellness to attack our tables. Generally speaking, we know what it takes to stay in good shape: eat the right foods, stay away from harmful substances like drugs and alcohol, engage in some kind of exercise every day, and get enough sleep each night. When we don't do those things for a prolonged period of time, we open the door to some pretty terrible consequences. Cancer. Heart disease. Diabetes. Autoimmune diseases.

Major medical problems can wreak havoc on your table. They drain your finances. They sap your strength. They cut into the time you have for work and relationships. They cause doubt and despair in your spiritual life.

Now, am I saying it's your fault if you have a major health concern? Am I blaming you for your issues? Am I saying that

God has work
for us to do
at every age.

God is punishing you by making you endure a difficult sickness? No. I'm not saying any of those things. Bad things happen to each of us, and each of us has a body that will eventually run out of juice. We are all walking around in temporary temples.

But. But! Even if we can't control everything about our health, we can control some things. And if we do a poor job of stewarding our bodies, then we are creating an opening through which our enemy can attack our tables.

And even destroy them. Destroy *us*.

SATAN WANTS TO END YOUR EFFECTIVENESS

A few years back my personal trainer put me on a machine that was supposed to measure my body's "real age." I was thirty-eight at the time, and that machine put me through several different tests. It measured my height and my weight. It measured my body fat. It measured my heart rate as I walked and ran, and a bunch of other stuff.

When all the tests were done, I got the answer back on my "real age." It was fifty-seven! I hadn't even reached my fortieth birthday, and this machine was telling me I had the body of a man on the verge of retirement.

I was shocked. In some ways, I felt like I had wasted nineteen years of my life.

Here's the bottom line: Satan not only can make us less effective at carrying out our assignments by attacking our physical health but also can end our ability to fulfill our purpose if we die before our time. Heart attacks. Strokes. Cancer. Organ failure. When our bodies fail, so does our ability to steward our tables.

You want to hear something scary? In 2010, the average life

expectancy for a US citizen was 78.7 years. Almost 80. By 2021, though, life expectancy dropped to 76.1 years.[6]

Here's the really scary part: There are about 350 million people in America. That means collectively, as a country, we've lost more than a billion years of productivity because of shortened lifespans. More than a billion years of people investing their time and talent and energy into making the world a better place.

Of course, medical issues are not the only way Satan can attack our bodies. There are also addictions and overdoses. There are drunk-driving accidents and homicides. There's suicide. Whatever the devil can do to knock you out of alignment with God and cut you off from your assignment, he will do. He is a roaring lion, always on the prowl.

The bottom line is that Satan wants to attack us through our health. When we let him, we end up losing our most precious gift of all: time.

Your Body Needs Helpful People

You probably know the drill by now when it comes to the final section of these chapters.

In chapter 2, I said to invite people to your table who can help you manage and maximize your resources—specifically, to invite people who understand your assignment and can contribute to your goals. In chapter 3, we saw that your table needs spiritually healthy people who can support you and keep you accountable. In chapter 4, we saw that you need people at your table who can offer a listening ear and a truthful tongue to help maximize your mental health.

Now, as we finish this chapter, I want to make the point that you need people at your table who can help you do an awesome job of managing your body and maintaining your physical health. This isn't a suggestion. This isn't just a good option. You *must* have people in your life who can support you when it comes to strengthening and extending your life.

What kinds of people? First, you need a good doctor. You need a medical professional—like a primary care physician—who knows their stuff, who knows you as a person, and who knows how to explain medical information in a way you can understand. This needs to be someone you trust. Someone who genuinely wants you to be healthy—not someone who sees you as a meal ticket or just another face in the crowd.

Here are a few questions you should ask yourself when it comes to finding the right doctor to speak into your life:

- Does my doctor know my name? Do they recognize me when I come in the room?
- Does my doctor listen to what I say? Do they hear me when I describe my symptoms, or do they just get out the prescription pad and tell me to try the next pharmaceutical?
- Does my doctor have time in their schedule to fit me in? Am I able to make appointments in a reasonable amount of time?
- Does my doctor understand nutrition? Do they recognize the connection between what I eat and how I feel?
- When I listen to my doctor and do what they say, does it help? Do I get better?

Of course, the best doctor in the world won't extend your life by a millisecond if you never pick up the phone and make an appointment. That's a problem for many people—especially many men. We don't want to go to the doctor, so we just keep putting it off, saying, "Not today. Maybe in a couple of months." But when a couple of months turns into a couple of years, or even a couple of decades, that's a problem. That's an invitation for Satan to do some damage in your life.

Being a good steward of your physical health means visiting your doctor every year for a checkup. It means consulting your doctor when something's not right with your body or when your body is changing in a significant way. And it definitely means doing what your doctor says—following their advice and taking your medicine.

What other people should you have at your table in addition to a trusted doctor? I think a personal trainer is a helpful option. My trainer certainly has been helpful for me, and I still meet with him regularly even though I've been working out on my own for years. Why? Because he knows things I don't know, and he helps me see things I don't currently see. He is an important voice speaking into my physical health, so I make time to hear what he has to say and watch what he wants to show me.

A nutritionist can be another helpful option for maintaining and maximizing our physical health. The human body runs like most complex machines: When you put good fuel in the tank, you'll get good performance from the engine. But when you put in the wrong type of fuel or the wrong amount of fuel, you'll have trouble. Things won't work the way they were designed to work.

The problem is that many of us don't feel confident when it comes to identifying and eating the right types of fuel for our bodies. There are so many fads out there and so many opinions flying around that we can easily feel confused. *Are eggs good for me or bad for me? Should I buy organic produce? What is gluten, and do I need to stop eating it?*

A nutritionist can help you put together a plan for fueling your specific body. You'll understand *what* to eat but also *why* certain foods affect you in certain ways. You will literally become an informed consumer, and your health will benefit (which means your table will benefit).

Whatever direction you take, I strongly recommend you identify at least a couple of trustworthy individuals who have the knowledge and capacity to help you steward your body well—to help you maintain (and even improve) your physical health. You need those people as part of your team because you need your body as part of your table.

Once you find the right people, make the invitation. Be direct about inviting them into your life, and be specific about sharing the goals you are asking them to help you achieve.

Your body will thank you for it in the years to come!

CHAPTER 6

A HEALTHY CAREER

W ell, that was one of the more interesting meetings I've ever had."

I was having lunch with a friend several years back, and I remember she had kind of a dazed look on her face when she walked into the coffee shop. She didn't say hello, which wasn't like her. She just sat down and went right into describing this meeting.

"This was a meeting with your boss, right?"

She nodded. "We spent half an hour talking about the trajectory of my life."

"Trajectory of your life?" That sounded like a weird phrase to hear from a boss. "What does that mean?"

"Well, he walked me through what's going to happen in my career. Like, I should work for so many years, then pursue this promotion, then push for this position. He told me where I could end up if I keep working hard for the next thirty years."

"That's a long time," I said.

She nodded again. "But it wasn't just my work. He told me how things would go if I chose to have kids—like, how that would affect different options at work. He told me when I could hope to retire. It was a lot."

"He told you all this?"

"Yeah."

She seemed pretty chill about the whole thing, so I asked again. "*He* told *you* about *your* life?"

"Yeah." She had caught the tone in my voice, and now she sounded like she was asking me a question. "Why?"

"He *told* you about your life?"

"Yeah . . ." Now she seemed confused. Maybe even a little worried.

"How does that make you feel?"

"I mean," she said, "it wasn't a big deal in the meeting. But now that you're saying it this way, I guess he never asked me what I wanted. He never asked what I planned to do about kids or promotions or retirement or any of that. He just told me where I'm going."

She was quiet for about a minute, and I let her sit and think. Finally she said, "I don't like that."

"I don't like it either," I said. "You're the one who needs to decide what happens with your life."

We talk a lot about work in our culture, and rightfully so. When you think about it, we spend the majority of our lives either working or sleeping. That's true no matter what type of work you do in a given week, whether it's clocking in from nine to five, running a business, freelancing at odd hours, or working all day as a stay-at-home parent.

All of us are working. All of us are investing a huge percentage of our time, our energy, and our other resources into this thing we call "work."

The question is, How does our work fit with our tables? What's the relationship there—and what *should* that relationship look like as we pursue lives of abundance, wellness, and freedom? Those are the kinds of critical questions I want to address in this chapter.

Your Work Is Not Your Table

When it comes to this relationship between your work and your table, the first thing to know is that those two terms are not the same. Meaning, your work is not your table. Your work is not your life, even though some of us can get a little confused on that connection.

Let's make sure we're on the same page for those terms. We've already seen that your table is your life. Your table is everything you've been given by your Creator in order to complete His assignment for your life. That means every person from the least to the greatest has a table they are called to steward.

What about work then? Most of us connect the concept of work with whatever we do to earn a living. Meaning, we mostly think of our work in terms of what we do to get paid. But that doesn't apply in all situations. Stay-at-home parents do a heck of a lot of work, for example, but they don't get paid for it. There are also a few people who don't seek jobs because they're already financially secure; they have all the money they need. Even so, I would say those people still have work that they do.

Here's a quick definition: Wherever you invest a large part of your waking hours, that's your work. If you have a job you do for thirty-five or fifty or seventy hours every week, that's your work. If you're a full-time student, then learning is your work. If you're a philanthropist who spends your time giving money rather than earning money, then that's your work. And if you take care of your family every day, that is certainly your work as well.

I want to make this clear: The reason your work isn't the same thing as your table is because your table is connected to your God-given assignment—but the work you do may *not* be related to your God-given assignment. In fact, I believe many people have work that is actually a distraction or a detriment when it comes to their assignments. The work they have chosen to do pulls them away from their assignments rather than contributing to their assignments—which is a problem.

So let's start right there. My goal for this chapter is to help you approach your work and career in a way that supports your table rather than detracts from it. To do that, I want to look at two common ways that our work brings harm to our tables. Once we've explored those negative examples, then we'll take a deeper look at how our work can help us maximize our tables instead.

WHEN YOUR WORK BECOMES THE HEAD

The first way our work can damage our tables is when that work determines the direction of our lives. In other words, we harm ourselves when we allow work to sit at the head of the table.

Now, we already talked a little about this in chapter 2 in terms of allowing a boss (or bosses) to claim a seat at the head of our tables. That is a bad idea on many levels because, as I mentioned to my friend in the earlier story, you and I were created by God and called by God to sit at the head of our tables. You and I have been assigned to manage the direction of our lives.

I want to be clear about this once again because it's important for anyone who has a "regular" job: Having a boss is not a bad thing. Having a boss who is interested in your life is not a bad thing. It's very possible to have a boss sitting at your table in a way that contributes positively to your life.

That's what I try to do with my team members. When I hire someone for one of my businesses, I do everything I can to ensure they are in line with my assignment in life and that they have the skills and wisdom and personality necessary to help me maximize my table. At the same time, I do everything I can to make sure that *I* will be able to support and contribute to *their* tables. Yes, I am their boss, but I also want to have a positive impact in their lives. I want to participate in their tables in a way that helps them fulfill their assignments.

Again, it is common and perfectly normal for your boss to sit at your table in a way that produces positive things. That's how it should be.

How can you tell when your boss is bringing harm to your table? When they start to steer your life or influence you in directions you don't want to go. When they assert control in a way that limits your ability to achieve abundance, wellness, and freedom. That's when you know there's a problem.

Now, obviously, I'm not talking about healthy workplace boundaries or regulations. If you tell me your boss is limiting your freedom because she won't let you take off every Friday as a paid vacation day, you're not going to get any sympathy from me. In any company, policies and procedures must be in place to help everyone be productive for that company.

But if your job or your boss begins to pull you away from

your God-given assignment—or if your career makes it difficult or impossible for you to fulfill that assignment—then something must change. That is an unhealthy situation that needs to be resolved.

The other way your job can get pushed to the head of your table is when *you* put it there. Meaning, you start to make all your decisions and determine all your priorities to benefit your career rather than your assignment.

What we often call workaholism is a good example. People who sacrifice their health or the wellness of their families in order to work long hours, push for promotions, and generally make work the most important thing in their lives are causing damage to their tables because they care more about their careers than they do about their assignments.

Let me say this while we're on the subject: Your immediate family should be the primary beneficiary of your table—not your job. Not your boss. When you're a spouse or a parent, your family should receive the main plate from your work, your effort, and your investment in your calling. Not the leftovers.

If your job is causing harm to your family because it deprives them of your presence, then you've put that job at the head of your table, and something needs to change.

WHEN YOUR WORK BECOMES THE FOUNDATION

The second way work can cause damage to our tables is when our jobs or careers become the foundations of our tables. When everything we are and everything we hope to achieve are dependent on maintaining that career or that paycheck, we have put ourselves in a dangerous place.

Earlier I mentioned working for a bill collection agency in California (DCB Associates). I got that job after dropping out of college, so I was working there when I turned twenty-one. Up to that point in my life, I had followed the law when it came to alcohol. Never touched the stuff. That was a choice I made in obedience to my parents and also because of my faith (even though my faith was a little shaky at the time).

Well, on my twenty-first birthday, my boss took me out to dinner at Applebee's. There was a special that night: five-dollar drinks. He bought me a couple of Coronas to celebrate my special occasion. Then a couple of Long Island iced teas. Remember, this was my first experience with alcohol in any way, and I became inebriated pretty quickly. Before long, I was drunk.

That's when my boss asked me some questions that were way out of line. Personal questions. And being young and inexperienced and drunk for the first time, I answered those questions in ways that were both honest and stupid. I said some things I never should have said—and never *would* have said if I were sober.

The next morning, I came into work (struggling with my very first hangover) and learned I had been fired. Just like that. What I'd said the night before had offended my boss, and he put in the paperwork as soon as he could. I was done.

That entire experience shook me in a major way, and not just because it was my first time being fired. No, it shook me because I had built my whole life around that job. My identity was wrapped up in being the star employee at that company—including all the promises of promotions and pay raises.

More practically, my finances were completely dependent on my salary. I had made purchases with that salary in mind, believing it would always be there.

In short, I had built my table on the foundation of that job—of that expected career. So when that job was taken away, my table was in danger of crumbling.

As I've gained experience in life, I've learned that nobody other than me or my spouse should have that much power over my table. Nobody else should be able to shake my table simply by removing themselves from it. Not a boss. Not a client. Not a company owner. Not a friend. Not even a parent or family member.

In a similar way, nothing should serve as the foundation of my table except my God-given assignment. Not my career. Not my financial goals. Not my personal reputation.

The same is true for you. Build your table to suit your assignment. Everything you add to your table ought to add naturally to your assignment.

That includes your work.

Your Work Contributes to Your Table

Your work is not your table. Your job is not your life. But your work and your job are *part* of your table. Your work and your job should contribute to your life in ways that help you fulfill your God-given assignment.

What does that look like? Speaking practically, it starts with money. The main reason most of us find a job is to earn a paycheck. We need financial resources to fuel and equip everything else connected with our tables. And that's okay. Working *only* for a paycheck is a poor way to approach your career. But appreciating your paycheck is always a good idea because your finances are a critical part of your table. (More on that in the next chapter.)

So, at the very bottom level, your work should contribute financial stability to your table. Your work should support your needs and provide the flexibility to pursue your passions and fulfill your assignment in your nonworking time.

Let me interject a couple of important things here. For one, there are times in life when we have a job that's just a job—and that's okay. The goal is to have a career that allows you to earn money as you fulfill your assignment, but not everyone gets to start there. Sometimes we just need a way to get food on the table and a roof over our heads.

This is especially true when you're starting out. I meet a lot of young people who feel frustrated because they're not "making a difference" with their work. They're working at Starbucks. Or in retail. Or at McDonald's. Or they're a junior assistant at some corporation where they do nothing but fill out spreadsheets and get coffee for the boss.

I understand the frustration with those situations. I've been there. But it's important to use that frustration as a motivator to move upward. If your job is just a job, don't get angry. Don't get disheartened. Don't get lazy or bored or apathetic.

Instead, get going! Use your current position as a stepping stone toward something better.

Second, you need to be aware of situations where your job is actually pulling you away from your assignment. You need to be on the alert for signs that your work is making you less effective or less able to fulfill your assignment. In those cases, find a way to move on as quickly as possible.

That's where I found myself with DCB Associates, even though I didn't know it at the time. My assignment is to help people—to educate and equip people with tools to help them excel in their finances. So banging on the phones for eight hours a day as a bill collector wasn't helping me pursue my purpose. The opposite was true. It made me cynical toward the very people I've been called to help.

So, in hindsight, I can see that being fired from that position was a blessing in disguise. Big-time. God used that moment to set me free from a season of work that was drawing me away from what He designed me to accomplish.

Okay, let's review again real quick: At the very least, your work should contribute to your table by providing wages. Hopefully your work also provides additional benefits and resources that help you manage and expand your table—healthcare, for example. Life insurance. Tuition assistance. A retirement plan. Paid vacation and sick leave.

The next level up is when your work provides fulfillment. This is when you feel good about the work you do—when that work has a purpose beyond a paycheck. Sometimes people describe this as the difference between a *job* and a *career*. When you enjoy what you do each day, you rise to a whole new level in terms of abundance, wellness, and freedom.

Incidentally, this is why so many stay-at-home parents can feel at peace about their work even without a paycheck. They see the value in the investment of their energy, and they enjoy

Be aware of
situations
where your
job is actually
pulling you
away from your
assignment.

the opportunity to spend most of their time with the people they love most.

Finally, your work really contributes to your table when it aligns well with your God-given assignment. When you receive compensation to do something that not only feels meaningful but also addresses your core purpose in life—that's the sweet spot. That's a life of abundance, wellness, and freedom.

I love it when people come up to me and say, "I can't believe I get paid to do this!" I know exactly how they feel. I've been feeling that way ever since I started my own businesses and realized I could earn way more money than I ever dreamed simply by being myself and doing exactly what I was born to do.

If you haven't reached that level yet, don't give up. Don't get discouraged. You have a God-given assignment, and you have the ability to align that assignment with the work you do each day. It may take some time. It may take a few sacrifices. You may have to move from one stepping stone to another as you work your way toward that goal.

But it can happen. It *will* happen. Just keep moving forward.

You Work Best When You Own It

One of my big fears in writing this book is that readers such as yourself will hear me say you have to be an entrepreneur in order to successfully manage your table. I'm worried people will hear me say you have to own your own business to experience abundance, wellness, and freedom.

Those things have been true for me because I was designed to be an entrepreneur. I am filled with abundance, wellness, and freedom every day because I have finally figured out how to connect my work with my assignment in a way that maximizes everything in my table.

I want the same thing for you, but I want to make it clear that your path won't be the same as my path. Each of us has a unique assignment, and we need to build our tables around that assignment if we want to find true meaning and purpose.

So let me say this once again just to be clear: It is absolutely possible to successfully manage your table and fulfill your assignment with a "regular" job. In fact, I strongly believe God has specifically designed and called most people to be great employees. (Meaning, it's perfectly possible for your current job to line up well with your assignment.)

If that's you, then own it. Make your job part of your table, and do everything possible to connect your work with your assignment so you are investing in your own fulfillment every time you show up at the office. Give your boss a place of honor and respect at your table, so long as you remain at the head. All of that is good and healthy.

But let me say one more thing: Even as you own your role as an employee, I also encourage you to own something else on the side. I'm talking about an income source that you own and manage for yourself. A side hustle.

Why do I recommend that? First, because ownership brings freedom. When you own something that produces revenue, all of a sudden you will see doors opening in your life that used to be closed. Opportunities will arise that would otherwise never have materialized.

Look at your own life right now, for example. Let's say you

have a good job and are happy in your career. You are satisfied. That's great. But would your life change for the better if you had an extra thousand dollars a month? What about five thousand? Or twenty thousand? Would those financial resources create a new level of freedom for you?

I remember the first time I hit six figures in my savings account. I was working for Ramsey Solutions at the time, so I was making good money, and I did a relatively good job of spending below my means. Pretty soon I had a substantial amount set aside for a rainy day. (This was separate from my retirement accounts.)

Do you know what that savings account gave me? Freedom. Abundance. I went to work each day with a different attitude—a new level of confidence. I was able to enjoy my work more because I wasn't dependent on that work to meet all of my immediate needs. I had some cushion. In fact, I realized that if I were to lose my job for some reason, I could spend the next year living roughly the same lifestyle without any problem. I could still date when I wanted. I could still head to the barbershop every week. I could even maintain my country club membership and keep playing golf!

Those extra resources were more than money in the bank. They put freedom in my pocket. And when I started to feel like it was time for me to move on and start a company of my own, I wasn't constrained by my salary. I was able to let go of a dream job in order to grab hold of a God opportunity.

The second reason I recommend that nine-to-five employees create their own side hustle is because ownership brings security. Remember, it's never a good idea for someone other than yourself or your spouse to have control over your table. That includes your boss—even if you like your boss. Even if your boss is a wonderful person. Because you know what? Bosses can retire or be replaced. Situations can change. And if the stability of your table is dependent on a company providing you a job and a salary, then you are in a precarious position.

Again, let's look at your life. If you were to lose your job tomorrow, what would happen to your financial situation? To your family? To your lifestyle? If you are currently dependent on a paycheck to make ends meet, you could be in real trouble once that paycheck is no longer available.

But if you control some of your own paycheck, you will have more security. You might not be comfortable—you probably wouldn't be able to replace your entire salary through your side hustle—but you would have more stability. You would have extra time to figure out your next step.

Right now you might be thinking, *I see your point, Anthony, but I don't know how to create a side hustle. Where would I even start?*

Well, start with your assignment. Start with your talents and your areas of passion. There are plenty of opportunities out there for anyone willing to take advantage of them.

The tech industry is a great example. My web designer is a young man who works a regular job and builds websites on the side. I paid him thousands of dollars to create my website, and I pay him $500 a month to maintain everything. For him, it's all on the side. It's all gravy. But it's good money that supplements his full-time job.

But Anthony, I'm not qualified! There are hundreds of

Those extra
resources put
freedom in
my pocket.

tech boot camps and certifications available online. You can spend six weeks getting educated and even licensed to do any number of jobs, and then you can get to work. Right away. You can invest as much time and energy as you like and reap as many rewards as you are able. No need to wait four years for a degree.

The content creation industry is another great example of a field ripe for harvesting. That includes YouTube, social media, copywriting, infographics, podcasts, webinars, marketing, ebooks, and much more.

Maybe you're scoffing a little at that direction, but the content creation industry is expected to generate more than $70 billion in annual revenue by 2030.[1] To put that in perspective, the total revenue for the National Football League was $11.98 billion in 2022.[2] So content creation is a huge pie that's getting huger, and you have the opportunity to get your own slice.

Again, you have so many options for starting a side hustle. Here are just a few thoughts that may spark your own ideas:

- If you're a people person, start an Uber or Turo business in your free time. You'll get some great tax write-offs, you'll meet lots of new people, and you'll earn extra income.
- If you're a teacher and you never want to leave the classroom, use this coming summer to develop video courses that help train new teachers. You can sell those courses to earn extra income *and* help the next generation get started well.
- If you're a construction worker, a plumber, or an electrician, find a way to buy a discounted home and then spend

a year flipping it in your spare time. When you're done, you can either sell it or rent it out for passive income.

Here's my point: Even if you love being an employee, find a way to own something as part of your overall financial picture. That is a great way for your work to contribute to your table.

CHAPTER 7

FINANCIAL WELLNESS

I remember the first time I saw you on Dave Ramsey's show. I thought to myself, *Who is this Black man? It feels good to see someone who looks like me on this platform.*"

That's what one of my listeners said about the first time she heard about me and started listening to me. Then she told me her story, which I thought was amazing. I'd like to share that story with you here because it's a good picture of how you and I should approach our money as an important part of our tables.

This woman—I'll call her Keisha—was pretty honest in sharing that she started watching my show because she could relate to me a little more than other financial thought leaders. Because I'm Black and because of the way I communicate about money, she could tell we came from the same place, both geographically and culturally.

Keisha started listening to me about five years before we met, and right away she made some big changes to her financial life. She got rid of all her consumer debt. She became serious about her budget. She established an emergency fund.

"Ever since I started following your advice," she told me, "I've been able to save about $12,000 a year. Every year."

It's a good thing too. A little while ago, Keisha's mom got sick and needed round-the-clock care. This was especially scary because Keisha lived in Southern California, while her mom lived in North Carolina. They were separated by an entire continent.

By that time, Keisha had about $80,000 in the bank. She knew what she needed to do.

"When I walked into my boss's office to hand in my resignation, I thought I would feel afraid," she told me. "But I wasn't scared. I had a plan, and I knew I could follow it."

"What did you feel?" I asked her.

"I felt confident," she told me. "I felt free."

Keisha quit her job and sold her home. She made about $180,000 in profit from that sale, and she put $20,000 of that into her savings to make an even $100,000. The rest she moved into a down payment for a home in North Carolina—one that was big enough for her and her mom. After her down payment, the mortgage was only about $1,600 a month.

"As soon as I finished moving Mom into our new space," she told me, "I took $20,000 out of my savings account and paid my mortgage for a whole year."

Then she got to work helping her mom get better. Her mom received a social security check every month, which helped cover utilities and food. But otherwise Keisha took care of everything—including the person that mattered to her most.

I love that story because it shows the power of the three big themes we've been talking about throughout this book. Because Keisha had been saving for several years, she had the *freedom* to walk away from her job and her home when something important came up. That freedom allowed her to make her mom's *wellness* a priority; it also allowed Keisha to cover her own needs and maintain her lifestyle even when she temporarily stepped away from her career. Finally, Keisha was able to bless her mother and spend a significant amount of time with her every day during a period of need, which is definitely a picture of *abundance* in my book.

Freedom, wellness, and abundance. That's what we're striving for as we seek to fulfill our God-given assignments during our time in this world. And that's exactly what we can find when we steward our tables well.

Now, as we have come to what might be the most important chapter in this book, I want to show you that doing a good job of stewarding your table often depends on your ability to manage your money and maintain your financial health.

The Notorious B.I.G. said, "Make the money. Don't let it make you."[1] There's wisdom in those words!

We're going to look together at the ways money can impact our lives and our well-being. But first let's get on the same page about what money is and why money matters.

Your Money Is a Resource

Back in chapter 6, I said your job is not your table, but it should—ideally—contribute to your table. In a similar way, your money is not your life—but it should make a big impact *on* your life.

Or maybe I should say that a different way: The abundance or scarcity of your money *will* make an enormous impact on your life and on the lives of others.

The more I talk with folks out in the world, the more I

We're striving for freedom, wellness, and abundance as we seek to fulfill our God-given assignments.

believe there are two kinds of people when it comes to money. The first are those who feel pulled toward money. They need it, they can't get enough of it, and they're willing to do just about anything to get it. The second are those who feel repelled by money. They understand that money is a necessary part of life, but they don't like it. They don't want to be associated with it in any kind of meaningful way.

Now, you and I both know that first impulse can get us into trouble, especially when taken to an extreme. The Bible says, "The love of money is a root of all kinds of evil" (1 Timothy 6:10). We've been told since we were little kids that being greedy is wrong. That hoarding money is wrong. That living for money is wrong.

Before Jim Carrey was a famous actor, he used to walk around with a check for $10 million in his wallet. Not a real check. This was a check he wrote to himself. It was basically a way of reminding himself to bank on his talent. He believed in his heart that if he kept working and kept investing everything he had into his career, he would be able to cash that check one day.[2]

He was right. He made $10 million for the movie *Dumb and Dumber.* He got that paper he'd spent so much of his life dreaming about.

Then, not that many years later, Jim Carrey said this to an interviewer in Canada: "I think everybody should get rich and famous and everything they ever dreamed of so they can see that that's not the answer."[3]

Personally, I've been around enough millionaires to know money doesn't bring happiness. Money doesn't bring fulfillment or purpose, and money doesn't solve all your problems.

So that first way of thinking about money—being pulled toward money and wanting it more than just about anything else—is unhealthy. It's not a good way to live, and it's not an effective way to steward our tables. Most of us really do understand that deep down.

But what most of us don't understand is that the second way of viewing money—being repelled by it or trying to avoid wealth because we find it distasteful—is also unhealthy. Rejecting money is not a good way to live, nor is it an effective way to steward our tables.

I see this mindset especially in the church. Many people believe that loving God means hating money—that being faithful to God and living as a "good Christian" means not being stained or tainted by things that are financially complicated. This is not a helpful approach, and thinking that way can actually become harmful too.

What are you talking about, Anthony? Are you saying that choosing to keep my distance from money is a bad idea?

Yep. That's what I'm saying.

Fish live in a world made of water, which means they need to navigate life underwater. Birds live in a world made of air, which means they need to navigate life in the atmosphere.

As human beings, we live in a world of money. Our society is connected by an uncountable number of financial transactions and interactions that happen every single moment of every day. Buying food. Paying bills. Financing a home. Managing debt from your past decisions. Managing investments to try to make a better future. Interest rates. Mortgage rates. Credit card rates. Gas prices. Inflation. Savings accounts. Checking accounts. Debit cards. Online shopping. Free shipping. Salaries. Bonuses. Hourly wages. Federal taxes. State taxes. Local taxes. Sales taxes. Real estate taxes.

I could keep going, but do you get my point? We live in a world made of money, which means we need to become excellent managers of our finances. We need the ability to manage money well as a key part of our tables.

You might ask, "Anthony, if we're not supposed to be pulled toward money, and if we're not supposed to push money away, then what's the right answer? What is the correct approach to take toward money?"

Money is a tool. That's the bottom line. Our finances are some of the most important resources that make up our table. So we need to fall somewhere in the middle: not running away from it but also not desperate to have it and to hoard it.

Jim Carrey said money isn't the answer, which is true. Another man said, "Money isn't everything, but the lack of money can destroy everything."[4] Which is also true.

Money doesn't define you or set your value as a human being, but not understanding how to handle money may prevent you from reaching your full potential. Money won't get us into the kingdom of God, but money can help us build the kingdom. Money doesn't answer our burning questions, but as a resource, it can help us find the answers we need to fulfill our assignments.

See what I mean? Money is nothing more than a tool. But it's a useful tool.

So let's dig a little deeper into how to use it well.

Money is a
tool. That's the
bottom line.

Your Money Needs Vision

Whenever I talk about finances or financial planning or being a good steward of money, the very first thing I teach is the need for vision. Specifically, you need a vision for your life and a vision for your money.

The vision for your life is simply where you want your life to go. It's your goals. It's your five-year plan or twenty-year plan. It's your dreams or mission or purpose. Whatever you choose to call it, the vision for your life is the direction you plan to take your life in the short-term and long-term future.

That vision isn't necessarily one thing. It will include a list of plans or goals or steps. Here's an example of what a vision might look like for a young person in their twenties:

- Get married.
- Purchase a home before we have children.
- Launch my own business before I turn thirty-five.
- Raise three or four children.
- Start investing and saving for retirement.
- Travel every summer.
- Stay out of debt.

Obviously, that's not a complete plan because it's not for a real person. You want to be as specific as possible when you write out the vision for your life, and you want to emphasize the goals that are especially important to you and your family. (Like purchasing a home or traveling every summer.)

Here's another generic example of a vision for someone in their fifties:

- Help our kids achieve a college degree with no debt.
- Work twelve more years and retire at age sixty-five.
- Downsize to a smaller home after retirement.
- Maintain our current lifestyle after retiring, including traveling to see grandchildren.
- Set up a foundation for charitable work.
- Write a novel.
- Maintain a living will and have effective plans in place for distributing our estate in the event my spouse and I pass away.

That's what I mean by a vision for your life. It's not set in stone; things can bend and flex as your circumstances change. But everyone needs goals to work toward and a plan to achieve those goals in a reasonable amount of time.

One more important thing: Your vision should be in alignment with your God-given assignment. The plans you make for your life need to match your mission and purpose. So if God has called and equipped you to teach children and serve as a source of encouragement for upcoming generations, then a goal of retiring to a private island at age fifty-five would potentially be a problem. You don't want a clash between your assignment and that part of your plan.

Next, in order to be a good steward of your table, you need a vision for your money. This is your plan for making money, spending money, giving (sharing) money, and saving money. This plan should include both your needs in the present and your needs in the future. And that plan should definitely describe how you will spend less than you earn so you can have some margin in your financial life.

In other words, you need a budget. That's your vision for money.

Let's pause a moment to recap. To be a good steward of your table's financial resources, you need two things: a vision for your life and a vision for your money. Next, and most importantly, those two visions need to line up together. They need to match.

What do I mean? Well, look back at the young person's life plan I offered earlier. One of the goals on that plan was, "Purchase a home before we have children." That's a good goal. That's an important goal. But that's also a goal that will take some work to achieve—specifically, it will demand some saving. That person will probably need a down payment of 20 percent to purchase a home using a conventional loan. (If they qualify for an FHA loan, they would still need 3 to 5 percent.) So they will need that money to be available when the time comes to buy. Most people in their twenties don't have the ability to just whip up $50,000 or $75,000 to purchase a starter home.

For all those reasons, what would you say if you looked at that young person's budget and saw they were planning to save only $2,000 a year total? That would be a problem because they would have to wait twenty-five years *minimum* to put down $50,000 toward a $250,000 home.

To say it a different way, if the vision for your life includes purchasing a home, but the vision for your money doesn't include plans to save up for a down payment, you have a problem. The two visions don't match, which means your overall plan is worthless. You won't reach your goal.

Being a good steward of your finances is never easy, but it doesn't have to be complicated. It's certainly not impossible. It all starts with making a realistic plan for aligning your life goals with your money goals. Then comes the important work of following that plan, even when doing so is difficult.

There's one especially important key to managing your money, which is critical to your table: discipline.

Your Money Needs Discipline

The first time I saw my dream car, I was a teenager heading to Six Flags. I didn't even know at the time what kind of car it was, but as our family was driving down I-95 outside of Los Angeles, I was struck by the look of it. The other car was sleek. Powerful. Beautiful. I was practically drooling as my eyes followed it down the road and out of sight.

Ten years later, I was in my twenties when I saw my dream car again. This time I was able to study it for a bit because it was parked on the street. A Bentley. Still sleek. Still powerful. Still beautiful. In my eyes, it was the perfect automobile.

Later that week, I caught a ride over to the Bentley dealership. The closest one was just outside Beverly Hills, which was more than an hour away from my house. I didn't care. I made the trip and walked into the dealership like I owned the place.

Once again, I was stunned. Five or six Bentleys were lined up in the showroom. All the latest models. Each one was polished to perfection and gleaming in the overhead lights. I felt like a kid who had wandered into a candy shop.

This was the kind of showroom that didn't even put a sticker price on the floor models. You had to speak with someone to get that information. But I didn't need any numbers to know those cars were way out of reach for me. I was working my first real job at the time, but I spent just about everything I made. I was already carrying real debt and had no way to afford something so special.

I stayed in that showroom for a long time, just meandering from car to car. Nobody bothered me. In fact, I don't think anyone even noticed me.

Before I finally left, I made a promise to myself: *I'm going to buy one someday.*

Fast-forward another fifteen years, and I finally kept that promise. I bought my first Bentley, and I paid cash. How did I do it? Discipline. Literally, I saved money for five years before I made that purchase. By that time in my life I was making over six figures every year, so I could have taken out a loan. But I had also learned the dangers of debt and financing depreciating assets.

So I saved. Every paycheck, I set aside a little money for my dream car. And when I finally made the purchase, the feeling was amazing.

Unfortunately, I've been on both sides of the table (pun intended) when it comes to managing my finances. When I was a younger man, I spent periods of my life so deep in debt that I couldn't afford to do much of anything *except* work—work a little more and then keep working. I was deep in a hole and had to dig my way out.

More recently, and definitely since I began studying Dave Ramsey and his approach to finances, I've been able to make better choices. More disciplined choices. I've learned how to be a healthy steward of my finances.

Practically speaking, what does it look like to be disciplined with finances? Different answers will apply to different people depending on their differing financial situations. But here are some basic stages anyone can follow to get on the right path when it comes to effectively creating and managing a vision for their money.

STAGE 1: BUDGET TO LIVE BELOW YOUR MEANS

The very first thing you must do to get your financial house in order is to make a vision for your money that allows you to spend less than you make. If you make $5,000 a month net, plan to spend only $4,000—and then stick to that plan.

Also, don't take on any new debt. Stop using your credit card. Don't sign up for any new loans. Commit to spending less than you earn every single month, and then follow through. Be disciplined.

STAGE 2: SET ASIDE EMERGENCY SAVINGS

If you are starting from scratch with absolutely no sense about money, the next thing I would tell you is to open a high-yield savings account and save up one month of your net pay.

The main thing here is I want you to be able to cover at least one month of expenses. Again, every person's financial situation is different, but most of us will have these necessary expenses:

- Housing (rent or mortgage payment, insurance)
- Transportation (car payment, gas, insurance, and maintenance)
- Food (staples, not eating out)
- Medical insurance
- Utilities
- Day care or childcare (which may also include school tuition)

The idea here is that if you were to lose your job or suffer some kind of tragedy, your emergency savings could buy you at least a month's worth of time to figure things out. That might mean finding a new job, getting healthy (or getting out of the hospital), taking care of a loved one who is sick, and so on.

Also, the reason I include that last category is because it's very difficult to manage a crisis when you also have to manage your children. You don't want to put yourself in a position where you must choose between going to a job interview and taking care of your child. So build an emergency fund that includes what you typically spend in a month for childcare. (If you don't have children, then that budget amount would be zero.)

STAGE 3: PAY OFF ALL CONSUMER DEBT

For many people, this is the big obstacle. Debt is the big mountain on the path toward financial freedom that seems impossible to climb—impossible to conquer. But this obstacle must be conquered. This mountain must be climbed if you want to effectively manage your money.

You cannot be a good steward of your table if you are carrying debt. You must get rid of it.

What do I mean by *consumer debt*? It means any situation in which you owe money to a person or an organization because of a depreciating asset. If you have a car loan or a lease, that's consumer debt. If you have a credit card payment, that's consumer debt. The same is true for student loans, medical debt, gambling debt, and just about every other type of debt.

The only real exception for most people is a mortgage. When you buy a house, there's a good chance the house will appreciate over time—meaning it will make money just by sitting there—as opposed to a car, which loses value the moment you drive it off the lot. So I'm not too concerned if you are carrying debt for your home, although if you can get rid of that debt, you should.

You might be wondering, *Anthony, how in the world am I supposed to pay off my debt?* The best answer has been the same for decades: the debt snowball. This is the strategy Dave Ramsey made famous, and he has kept teaching it for so many years because it works. It is the most effective method you or I can use to get rid of our debt.

If you're not familiar with that strategy, the debt snowball just means paying off your debts one at a time, starting with the smallest one. For example, let's say you have these debts as part of your financial picture:

- You owe $187,000 on a thirty-year mortgage.
- You owe $13,000 on an automobile loan.

- You owe $3,650 on your Visa card.
- You owe $450 for a recent doctor's visit, which you've been paying off at $50 per month.
- You owe $7,500 in student loans.

The first thing you want to do for the debt snowball is arrange all these debts in order from the smallest to the largest. Don't worry about interest rates or how many years you have left on a payment plan or any of that. Just arrange your debts from smallest to largest.

In this example, that would be:

- You owe $450 for a recent doctor's visit.
- You owe $3,650 on your Visa card.
- You owe $7,500 in student loans.
- You owe $13,000 on an automobile loan.
- You owe $187,000 on a thirty-year mortgage.

Here's how the debt snowball works: Make the minimum payment on all of your debts except the smallest one. For the smallest one, do whatever you can to make an additional payment each month until it's gone. Let's say you can find an extra $100 each month to contribute toward your doctor bill. That means you'll pay $150 each month instead of only $50. After three months, that bill will be paid.

Now, here's the critical part. Instead of going back to normal, take that $150 and add it to your Visa payment every month. Instead of paying the minimum of $29, pay $179 every month until your Visa bill is paid off. Then take that extra $179 and apply it to your student loan payment every month, and so on. Keep building momentum—keep the snowball rolling—until all your debt is paid.

STAGE 4: EXPAND YOUR EMERGENCY SAVINGS

Once you've paid off all your nonmortgage debt, the next step is to funnel your extra money into building up your emergency fund. Specifically, I recommend you save enough cash to cover three months of your current income. If you're making $5,000 a month, for example, save until you have $15,000. You want to store up three months' worth of paychecks.

Why do I recommend saving three months of income rather than three months of expenses? Flexibility. If you were to lose a job or encounter a disability of some kind, your emergency fund would allow you to maintain your regular lifestyle for three months while you apply for a new job or seek a resolution. Or, if your situation were a little more desperate, you could stretch that emergency fund to last for five months by cutting back on everything except necessary expenses.

Here's an important tip: Don't save that money in a regular bank account that earns you .02 percent interest or some nonsense like that. Instead, put your emergency fund into a high-yield savings account that pays closer to 5 percent interest.[*] That way, if you have an emergency fund of $15,000 and leave it in a high-yield fund for a year, you'll earn an additional $750 over the course of that year without doing a thing.

---

[*] For helpful resources and recommendations related to your financial habits, check out www.AnthonyONeal.com/BookResources.

STEP 5: MULTIPLY YOUR MONEY

Once you get to a place where you have no debt and you've saved up an emergency fund to cover you for several months, you will be in a great place financially. You will have the stability and flexibility you need to manage your table well.

The next thing you can do is expand your table by multiplying your money. This is what we call wealth building: using your money to make more money and increase your margin.

Once again, each person should have a specific strategy for multiplying their money that matches their resources and the circumstances of their lives. But here are some general rules that everyone can follow to begin this process.

For starters, it's always a good idea to put away money for retirement. If your company offers a 401(k) benefit with a corporate match, take advantage of that match to the fullest extent possible. Save money in a Roth IRA, which allows you to pay taxes on the front end so you don't have to pay any additional taxes when you withdraw your money during your retirement. If you own a business, learn the value of a Simplified Employee Pension plan (also called a SEP IRA), which can enable you to transfer tens of thousands of dollars into your retirement every year as a business expense.

Beyond retirement, you may want to invest in the stock market through a brokerage account. Or purchase real estate. Or invest resources to expand your business or side hustle so it can generate greater revenue.

The basic idea is to invest your resources in ways that produce more resources. I can speak from experience when I say that expanding your financial portfolio is a fantastic way to expand the reach and impact of your table. The more you make, the more you can do.

Your Money Needs People

"Financial peace isn't the acquisition of stuff. It's learning to live on less than you make, so you can give money back and have money to invest. You can't win until you do this."[5]

Boom! Do you know who wrote those words? Dave Ramsey. The GOAT when it comes to personal finance for my generation. It still amazes me that I got to work with that man for seven years. Dave taught me so much during that time, and I feel responsible for passing on what I learned. That's one of the reasons I've written this book!

So let me pass along this important piece of wisdom: You need other people to help you manage your financial resources. You need good people at your table who can help you steward your money.

Specifically, I encourage you to gather what I call "the A-Team." You should invite these three types of people to your table, and their names all begin with *a*.

ACCOUNTABILITY PARTNER

The first person you should invite to your table is a financial accountability partner. This person will hold you to your financial goals, so it needs to be someone you are willing to talk with about those goals. This person should also be willing to tell you the truth—someone who will say, "I thought you were working to build that emergency fund, so why did you spend this much on that?"

Ideally, your financial accountability partner should be a little further along than you are in terms of their financial health. (Or this person could be a *lot* further along. That works too!) The goal is for you to have someone who can teach you what they've learned—someone who can answer your questions and provide some feedback or direction when you need it.

For example, Dave Ramsey was my accountability partner for years. He knew my goals. He had a good idea of my plans and priorities. And before I made any major purchase of any kind, I always ran it by Dave. "Hey, Dave, what do you think about this property?" Or "Hey, Dave, would it be a bad idea for me to buy a car right now?" Or "Hey, Dave, I am thinking about investing in this. What's your thought?"

I asked him all those questions and many more.

Now, you may not have access to a Dave Ramsey in your life, but you can have access to me. That's one of the reasons why I record *The Table with Anthony O'Neal*, and that's one of the reasons why I take live phone calls on my show. I want to be available to offer helpful advice when people in my E3 community (which includes you) have important questions—especially important financial questions. I want to help people *expand* in *three* areas: abundance, wellness, and freedom.

Other than myself, I do recommend you find an accountability partner who is familiar with your specific situation and who is willing to join you at your table.

ACCOUNTANT

The second person on your A-Team should be an accountant. An accountant may help keep track of your finances throughout the year, but their main job should be to assist you with taxes. Specifically, their goal is to help you legally and ethically pay the least amount of tax possible and to do so in the correct amounts each month or quarterly.

I hear from people all the time who say, "I'm so excited to file my taxes and get my refund. Last year I got $3,000 back!"

That's a bad tax plan. I know it seems as if you are "getting" that cash back when you pay your taxes, but the reality is you are only receiving back what you've been paying for twelve months. And the problem with a refund that large is that you've basically been giving the government a loan with no interest. You've been letting Uncle Sam hold on to your money for months when you could have been putting that cash to work for *you*.

A good accountant will keep your finances in order. With their help, you can pay the correct amount of tax—and keep more money in your pocket throughout the year.

ADVISOR

The third person on your A-Team should be a financial advisor. You want this person to be a professional—not a buddy. You want to find someone who knows what they are doing.

What does a financial advisor do? Using the language from earlier in this chapter, they help you match the vision for your life with the vision for your money. So a good financial advisor will spend a good bit of time asking you about your plans and your goals—your plans for yourself, individually, but also your plans for your family. Here are some examples:

- Buying a home within the next three years
- Starting a retirement account
- Sending your children to college debt-free
- Starting a business
- Purchasing a car
- Retiring by age sixty-five

Your financial planner will help you set up a budget that works and that produces margin in your money each month. Then they will help you use that margin to invest, save for retirement, multiply your resources, and follow a plan to match your vision for your money with your vision for your life.

Now, if you decide to start your own business, or if you reach a level in your finances that makes it necessary, you may want to add a fourth person to your A-Team. That would be an attorney. This will be necessary only if you want to set up and manage multiple LLCs, review contracts, seek legal advice, and so on.

Let me offer one final piece of advice before we close this chapter, and let me do it through a story. A few years ago in Nashville I took a woman to a nice restaurant for dinner. A fancy restaurant. We had a good time, and I was hopeful I'd have an opportunity to see her again.

Sure enough, she texted me a couple of days later: "How about a second date?"

With that text, she sent me a link to a different restaurant.

When I went to the website, I saw the pricing for the dinner she was suggesting was about $250 a plate—so $500 for the two of us.

I texted her back and spoke to her honestly. "I really enjoyed spending time together the other night, but this restaurant doesn't fit with my budget. I can't afford it."

"You can't afford it?" She seemed shocked. And maybe a little insulted.

Now, what she probably *thought* I was saying was that I didn't have enough money to cover the meal, which of course was not true. I had plenty of money in the bank.

What I meant, though, was that I could not afford for her expectations to derail my vision for my finances and my vision for my life. I could not afford such a large, unplanned expense because it would be irresponsible—not just in the present but for my financial future.

In other words, I had learned discipline. I had learned that just because I *have* money doesn't mean I need to *spend* that money. And I had learned that *my* plan for *my* money should always take precedence over what other people want me to do or expect me to do—and definitely over what the people around me say I'm supposed to do once I reach a certain level.

No more keeping up with the Joneses or the Gateses or the Beyoncés or anyone. You will be an effective steward of your table when you make a plan for your money and follow it through.

CHAPTER 8

RELATIONAL WELLNESS

I 've already raised two kids. I don't think I'm ready to start again."

This single sentence literally changed the course of my life. When I heard those words, I was in my therapist's office with my fiancée. We were in the middle of premarital counseling, and we were talking about our goals for the future. I was talking about my goals for raising children, and that's when she spoke honestly from her heart.

"I don't think I'm ready to start again. I don't want to be sixty-five and still waiting for kids to graduate high school."

To give some context, I met my fiancée when I was in my late twenties and she was in her early forties. She'd married young, had two kids, and divorced before she'd even heard my name. She'd endured the kind of life experiences that build wisdom. She was successful at her career. And she was smart. Basically, she was a fully mature woman just entering her prime.

On the other hand, I was a younger man still trying to figure things out for myself. In many ways I was a rising star in my field but still a little immature. Still growing. Still unaware of how much I didn't know.

Looking back, I should have approached her as a close friend—someone who could help me become the person I was created to be. But she was beautiful. Speaking honestly, she was one of the most stunning women I had ever met.

So I asked her out, and she accepted after my three attempts. And I kept asking her out, and she kept accepting. Pretty soon, I fell in love.

I should have popped the question that first year, but I was too insecure in my own position. Like I said before, she was very successful in her field, which meant she was making more money than I was. Quite a bit more money, actually. That caused me to feel uncertain about my role and my place as a man in our relationship. I wanted to be a strong provider, so I kept pushing things off. I kept waiting.

By the time I did ask her to marry me, we'd been together five years, which felt like a long time to both of us. We'd grown a lot closer during those years—but we'd also grown apart when it came to our dreams for the future. We had no idea our life goals had drifted until that moment in our counselor's office when she said out loud that she was done having children.

I wish I could say I handled that moment well, but I did not. The day after that difficult conversation at the therapist's office, I started another conversation with her that ended up leading to the end of our engagement. She had been the most important person in my life for several years, but I had determined in my mind to move on. So that's what I did—moved on.

Over the next several weeks, I convinced myself that I was handling things well. I played a lot of golf. I pressed into my career. I traveled more. I even went on a few dates.

Through it all, I just kept telling myself, *I'm fine. This is fine.* Which was a lie.

To make a long story short, I went into a season of depression without understanding what was happening. I didn't go see my counselor to talk about ending a relationship of five years. I didn't seek help from my closest friends and mentors. I just kept pushing forward, and I kept pretending everything was okay.

In hindsight, I can now see how the end of that relationship affected just about every other area of my life. I had trouble praying or connecting with God in a meaningful way. I spent money I shouldn't have spent trying to make myself feel better through activities and through dates with other women. I felt too tired to work out. I was distracted at the office. I pulled back from my family and my close friends.

Yes, I was eventually able to heal and find a path forward. But the impact of that single moment on every aspect of my life showed me then—and still shows me now—just how powerful relationships can be.

Let's take a deeper look at that power together as we explore the importance of relationships as part of our tables.

Relationships Are Part of Your Table

I know I've already said this about a hundred times in these pages, but the idea is important enough to repeat at least once more: Your table is your life. More specifically, your table includes everything your Creator has given you to fulfill your assignment. So your table includes your spiritual health, your mental health, your physical health, your work, and your finances.

Your table also includes your relationships.

Now, we need to make a separation here, because when I say

relationships, I don't mean the people you invite to your table to help you manage your resources and fulfill your assignment. I'm not talking about your doctor, your therapist, your financial advisor, and so on—the people you have specifically, intentionally invited to your table to help you.

Those people sit *around* your table. But your relationships are *part of* your table, just like your money or your physical body are parts of your table. I'm talking about all those relational connections that make up your life and influence you each day. Your relationships are your interactions with other people, both significant and insignificant.

That leads to an important principle: Your relationships are a resource in your life. Which means they need to be managed— and managed well.

Maybe you're wondering, *What relationships are you talking about specifically, Anthony? Which connections with which people?*

The answer is: all of them. With everyone. What I'm saying is that every relationship you have is a resource that should be included when you think about your table. That's because those relationships can have a huge influence on how effectively you manage your table and to what degree you fulfill your God-given assignment each day.

Start by taking stock of your closest connections. Your spouse or significant other. Your children. Your parents. Your siblings. Your closest friends. These are the most important relationships in your life, which means together they make up an important piece of your table.

Next are the relationships that are important or influential in your life but not as significant. That could include many of your friends and maybe a few of your coworkers. Maybe your boss. Also your neighbors, your pastor or small-group leader, your extended family members, your in-laws, the people you date, and so on.

Finally, your relationships also include acquaintances or loose connections. These are people who know you without knowing much about you. The delivery guy who brings packages to your doorstep. Old friends from high school that you haven't spoken with for more than a decade. The barista who recognizes you at your favorite coffee shop and remembers what kind of milk alternative you prefer. Your kids' teachers and coaches. That kind of thing.

All three of those levels are part of your overall relationships, and all three are important in their own way.

So what I'm saying is that you and I must steward our relationships in the same way we steward our money and our physical health. Our relationships are part of our table.

At the same time, our relationships are different from other pieces of our table (our money, our bodies, our minds, etc.). That's because our relationships have such a big impact on the quality and direction of our lives. You can have everything else in your life going for you—you're healthy, your job is great, your financial picture is strong, you love Jesus—but if a big conflict is raging between you and your spouse? Or your child? Or even your neighbor or your boss? All that good stuff can become tainted real quick.

Our relationships affect every other element of our lives. They are powerful.

I want to make one more point before we move to the next section in this chapter, and it has to do with the *quantity* of *quality* relationships in our lives. These days, most of us don't have much trouble making superficial connections. We've all got acquaintances. We've all got "friends" on social media. Anyone can pop over to a bar or a local church service and strike up a casual conversation. And don't even get me started on swiping left and right.

So the *quantity* of relationships is not a problem for most of us. What can be a problem, however, is the number of close relationships we enjoy. The quantity of our *quality* connections.

Why do I mention this? Because many people in our culture are lonely. Many people are lacking real, genuine connection with others—and things are only getting worse:

- In 1990 only 3 percent of Americans said they had no close friends.
- In 1990 33 percent said they had ten or more close friends.
- In 2021 12 percent of Americans said they had no close friends. Four times higher than in 1990.
- In 2021 only 13 percent said they had ten or more close friends.
- Today, one out of every three Americans has only two or fewer close friends.[1]

The reason this is a big deal is because loneliness is a big deal. In fact, a group of researchers did a study to figure out how harmful it can be to our physical health when we are lonely.

They discovered that the negative impact of loneliness on our physical health is the same as smoking fifteen cigarettes a day.[2] Fifteen a day!

Loneliness is killing us, which means it's more important than ever that we learn how to steward our relationships well. After all, if you lacked money as part of your table, that would be a problem, right? If you had no spiritual health, or if your mental health was severely lacking, those would be problems too.

The same is true for our relationships. When we don't have a significant number of significant people who are close to us and care about us, we can't manage our tables effectively. We will have a difficult time fulfilling our assignments.

Relationships Are the Point of Your Table

So far we've established that relationships are an important part of your table. But I would go further and say that relationships are *the point* of your table. Relationships are the reason you and I have been given a table and asked to steward it well.

This goes back to your assignment. Remember, God created you and equipped you with a table because He has a purpose for your life. He designed you to fulfill a specific mission—a specific assignment.

What we need to remember is that our assignments almost always involve people—which means our assignments require us to be in relationships.

Let's say I wanted to spend the next fifty years just living in a bunker and creating content. I'd have someone deliver my meals every day, but otherwise I would only work and sleep.

Relationships
are *the point*
of your table.

Let's say I took all the money I earned creating that content—which would be a significant amount, I'm sure—and donated all my profits to the poor. Every year, whatever I earned would go directly to charity.

Would that be a life well spent? Would that be a table well stewarded?

No. For one thing, I would be doing a lot of harm to myself because I'm a human being created to be in relationships with others. I'm built for connection.

More importantly, though, God didn't create me to make money. He doesn't need my help making money or generating resources! No, He created me to make an impact. He created me to make a difference. And I can't achieve those goals unless I establish meaningful connections with people.

The same is true for you.

It starts with your family. Your household. If you're married with kids, then you live every day in the middle of a mission field of infinite possibility. There is no limit to the difference you can make in the lives of those you love most. Spiritually. Physically. Emotionally. And yes, financially. You have the opportunity to serve and bless your favorite people when you invest in those relationships.

Next comes your community. This notion may seem strange, but I don't believe you're living where you're living by accident. I believe that all of us are called to our current homes in order to serve those we encounter there—in order to serve our communities.

Part of your community is geographical. Your neighborhood. Your condo association. Your city. You have been placed in a place, which means you have some responsibility to know the people around you. To connect with them. To care for them when care is needed. Obviously we can't interact with everyone, but we should all be making an effort to interact with someone each day. We should be on the lookout for ways to make a difference in line with our assignments.

Another part of your community is interpersonal. That includes your friends and coworkers. It includes your church congregation and definitely a small group (if you're part of one). It may include the people at your child's school or at least their teachers. There are so many people who move in a similar orbit to you each day, which means you have so many opportunities to reach out and make meaningful connections.

Doing a good job of managing the relationships at your table means taking advantage of those opportunities more often than not.

Here's something interesting I've observed during my life. I call it the 33/33/34 principle. If you were to make a list of every single person you know or interact with in a given year, I would guess that about 33 percent of those people are ahead of you in terms of their development and success at fulfilling their mission. About one-third.

You can learn from these people. They are potential mentors and guides. They can teach you a great deal if you are willing to learn.

The next 33 percent of people are on the same level as you. They are your peers. They may not be in the same career field as you or have the same values as you, but they are at a similar level of advancement in their lives.

You can both learn from and serve these people. They provide you with opportunities to gain wisdom and give wisdom. To seek help and offer help.

The final 34 percent of people on your list would be folks who are behind you in terms of their overall level of success. These people aren't worse off than you, and you're not more valuable than they are. But they may be younger or just starting out. Or they may have been forced to endure a few tragedies that delayed their development. For whatever reason, they would look at your life and see someone moving a little further ahead.

These are the people you can serve. These are the people you can teach and guide. In other words, these people represent the best opportunity for you to make an impact in your community.

Are you taking advantage of those opportunities?

Serving other people within the context of our assignments starts with our families, then expands to our communities—and then expands fully to our world. No matter what else you may be, you are a citizen of this planet. You are a runner in the human race. And that means you have a chance to make a difference.

Most of the time this means being one of the millions of people who take little steps that all add up to a big difference. Like recycling, for example. Or being an informed voter. Or being responsible with your taxes. Maybe for you that means leaving a big tip for a server just because you want to be nice. Or making room for people to merge on the highway. Or signing a petition for a cause you believe in.

The point is this: When enough of us take little actions because we care about the web of relationships that connects our world, we really can make an impact in that world. We really can make a difference.

Relationships Require Wisdom

It's time to revisit something I said at the beginning of this chapter. Earlier I made it clear that there is a difference between stewarding the relationships in your life and inviting people to join you at your table. And that's important. There is a difference, mainly because you don't have room at your table for every relationship in your life. Even every close or important relationship.

In my experience, though, it can be difficult to make a separation between the relationships you steward as *part of* your table and those people you invite to sit *around* your table. It's hard to keep the first group from bleeding into the second group. But it's also important to distinguish the difference, because when that happens—when the people you are close to assume they have a role in managing or directing your table—you will be less effective at carrying out your assignment.

Here's a principle: Just because you love someone does not mean they get a seat at your table. Just because you love someone (or just because they love you) does not mean they are automatically invited to offer you advice or instruction when it comes to stewarding your life.

Now, the exception is your spouse. I want to make that clear right away. When you join yourself to another person in a marriage relationship, you definitely bring them to your table—and you definitely take a place at their table. In many ways, you combine your tables into one when you take that step together.

Like the Bible says, "Therefore a man shall leave his father and mother and be joined to his wife, and they shall become one flesh" (Genesis 2:24 NKJV). When I visualize my table right now, for example, I am sitting at the head, but there's an empty seat on the other side. I have reserved the other seat of honor at my table for my wife, and she will take that seat the moment we become one.

So your spouse gets an automatic seat at your table, but that is not true of any other relationship. Once you're an adult and are managing your own life, your parents do not get an automatic seat at your table. Neither do your grandparents, your siblings, or your kids.

Why am I mentioning this? Because it's common for people to assume their loved ones—whether family or their closest friends—should naturally be able to provide input and direction in their lives. And I think that assumption goes both ways. Meaning, it's easy for someone like me to assume that my loved ones should have a seat at my table, and it's easy for my loved ones to assume they should have a seat at my table.

Please hear me: Both of those assumptions are wrong. Both of those assumptions can cause serious damage in our lives, including hampering or hindering us from fulfilling our God-given assignments.

I think this principle is hardest to accept when it comes to parents and their adult kids. In fact, I get pushback from moms and dads all the time when I suggest they should not insert themselves into their children's lives without being invited.

"Anthony, I raised that child for eighteen years. I know what's best for him."

"With respect, no you don't."

Hear me on this, parents. If you think you know what's best for your children, and if you are constantly stepping in to offer advice on the careers your children should pursue, how they should handle their finances, how they should treat their spouses, how they should raise their own children, and on and on—you are not loving them. You are not serving them.

Instead, you are preventing them from sitting at the heads of their own tables.

Likewise, if you as an adult allow your parents or anyone else to push you in this direction or that direction when it comes to the important decisions in your life, then you are not sitting at the head of your table.

Now, am I saying you should never ask your parents for advice or seek their counsel? Am I saying you should never invite your parents to take seats at your table? No. Not at all. But the keywords there are *ask* and *invite*. If you believe a parent or a close friend can help you maximize your table in a specific area and help you take another step toward fulfilling your assignment, then by all means, invite them to your table.

But the choice needs to be yours. Not theirs. There needs to be an invitation, and it needs to come from you.

In my own life, for example, I love my fathers—my Cali dad and my Carolina dad. Both of them are good, godly men. Both of them have always been strong, fair fathers who worked hard and sacrificed to bless their children, including me. So we love

The keywords

there are *ask*

and *invite*.

each other. In fact, at the risk of sounding corny, I believe my dads and I would take a bullet for each other.

But have I invited my fathers to join me at the table when it comes to building and managing a seven-figure business? No. Not because they don't love me but because neither of them has experience building or managing a seven-figure business. They don't have the expertise to help me expand my table in that way. So I don't ask them to help me. I bring others to my table who do carry that experience and that authority.

Now, when I do get married and have children of my own, will I seek advice from my fathers on being a good husband and raising my children well? Absolutely. I will invite them to speak into that area of my life because I know they can help me.

In a similar way, we need to be careful about allowing our close friends to take seats at our tables. I have some great friends I enjoy spending time with. We get together often to golf or work out or have a meal or just share life.

Those friendships are important. Those friendships are healthy. Those friendships are valuable and need to be stewarded well. Such relationships bless us, and they give us opportunities to be blessings in return. All of that is good.

But remember: Spending a lot of time with someone does not make them a good candidate to help guide and manage the direction of your life. Enjoying a person's company does not mean they should automatically receive a seat at your table.

What's my point here? I'm saying we need to be wise in managing our relationships, just as we need to be wise in managing our money, our time, our health, and so on. We need wisdom to know how to steward the relationships God has brought into our lives. We need wisdom to understand how to set boundaries when someone has invited themselves to our tables without our permission (more on that in the next chapter). And we need wisdom to learn how to love and care for those dearest to us—our families and our closest friends—without giving them access to our lives that is inappropriate or unhelpful.

Be wise in the ways you steward your relationships.

CHAPTER 9

THE IMPORTANCE OF AN OPEN TABLE

After I left Ramsey Solutions, I was anxious to prove myself. Actually, I was anxious to prove myself *to me*! I wanted to show others that I could be a success on my own, but I was equally motivated to show myself.

So I got to work.

The first thing I did was put together a video course called *The Single's Blueprint*. I knew from experience (my own and that of other singles) that our society tells single people to live it up during their years of freedom—that our "real life" doesn't start until we get married and raise a family. I also knew from experience that such a message is a lie. Real life is happening now, no matter what season you happen to be in relationally.

That subject had been on my mind for years, and I was excited to create something genuine. I was excited to offer something that could help people I'd never met maximize an important season of their lives.

It took a long time to put the content together, but I was patient and persistent. My team was smaller at the time, but we worked on the videos. We worked on the curriculum. We worked on the delivery system. We did everything we could to make the end product as useful and as easy to access as possible.

When it came time to launch the course, I felt almost crazy with anticipation. I truly believed in my product, I had worked hard, and now it was time to reap the benefits. Now it was time to show everyone I belonged.

The way we rolled out the course was to offer a free webinar that anyone could access and benefit from—a quality stand-alone. Then anyone who really connected with what we were offering could purchase the full course and take it all the way through. We had a lot of marketing in place to point people toward the webinar, but once they started watching, it was up to me and my prerecorded content to show them how valuable the full course could be.

As the numbers started rolling in, I was filled with optimism. Right away we had thousands of people watching the webinar. Then a couple thousand. By the end of the first week, more than ten thousand people had worked through the free video.

I'll admit it: I thought we were going to make a million dollars right out of the gate. Easy. I've always been confident in my capacity as a speaker. I've always relied on my ability to own the stage. So I figured most of those who watched the free webinar would convert to the full course pretty quickly. I was convinced we were at the beginning of a smash hit. A huge success.

I was wrong. By the end of the first month, the full course had generated only about $220,000 in revenue. That may seem like a big number, but you have to remember we'd spent a good amount of money producing the course. I also had team members relying on me for their salary. So the actual profit from the course fell way short of what I'd hoped.

Honestly, I felt like a failure.

Around that time I had a chance to speak with a friend of mine who'd been successful in the content creation space. I told him what had happened, and he agreed to take a look at what we'd created and give some feedback. What he said surprised me.

"You're a great communicator, Anthony. But a great communicator isn't the same thing as a great seller." That caught my attention. Wasn't selling just a form of communicating?

"What do you mean?" I asked.

"You inspired me during the webinar," he said. "You motivated me. You kept my attention. But you didn't show me the reason why I *needed* to purchase the course."

To make a long story short, I spent the next six months working with a sales coach. We started from the ground up and re-evaluated everything we'd been doing as a business to that point. He taught me how to sell from onstage. He taught me how to sell through YouTube. He taught me how to sell through lead magnets and other types of free content. He taught me how to use my own story to connect with people's felt needs.

Probably most importantly, he taught me how to show people my vision for the future—not just my future but theirs as well. He taught me how to open myself up spiritually and morally so people weren't just buying a product; they were buying *me*.

You know what? It worked. After those six months, we relaunched *The Single's Blueprint* and other courses and products through my new platform. Same audience, but much different results. In fact, after only a few weeks of selling the course in the new way, we passed that million-dollar benchmark. And we've continued to maintain that seven-figure sales range year after year as we create new courses.

That experience taught me many important lessons, and I'll share a few of them with you throughout this chapter. But the biggest thing it taught me was the importance of being open and flexible with my table.

Your Table Is Expandable

I don't know if you've noticed this, but it's easy for people to get comfortable being comfortable. It's easy for people to settle for what's always been there—to be satisfied with what they've always had.

This can happen with our daily routines, for example. We can settle into a pattern of getting up at the same time. Going to work at the same time. Eating the same thing for breakfast. Going to the same place for lunch. Spending the same amount of time at work and the same amount of time on break. Coming home at the same time and working through the same chores in the evening. Ending up on the same sofa and watching the same shows before going to bed at the same time and setting our alarms to start the whole thing over again the next day.

Routines aren't bad in and of themselves. Being comfortable isn't bad either. But if we're not careful, routines can turn into ruts. And comfort can cause us to close ourselves off from new adventures and new opportunities.

The reason I mention this is because it's possible to become comfortable with the state of our tables. It's possible to assume we'll always be at the same level of physical and mental health, that we'll always maintain the same relationship with God, that we'll always have the same job, that we'll always follow the

Routines can turn into ruts. And comfort can cause us to close ourselves off from new adventures and new opportunities.

same budget, and we'll always connect with and depend on the same relationships.

In my opinion, it's a problem when we close our tables in that way. Because there are some seasons when our tables need to grow. To expand. And since we were designed to grow and expand, it's harmful for us to become stale and stagnant.

Now, let me say first that not everyone is in danger of a rut. Not everyone has to worry about their tables becoming closed and rigid. Like me, for example. I am constantly looking for ways to expand. I am continually scanning the horizon to see what's out there and what could be next—continually searching for new opportunities to grow and new goals to conquer. That's just how I'm wired.

That's why I need people at my table who remind me to rest. "Anthony, you need to slow down," they may say. Or "Anthony, when was the last time you took some time for yourself?" Or "Bro, have you prayed about this step?"

So if you're built like me, you may have to learn when to step back from searching for what's new and say, "Enough is enough—at least for this season."

According to my experience, however, most of us encounter trouble amid our natural resistance to change. This is especially true when things are going well. When our lives are pretty good, we can be hesitant to take the risks that typically accompany expansion and growth. We can close ourselves off from new openings because of comfort or fear—or both.

Here's the big question I'd like us to consider together: *When do I need to expand my table?* In other words, how can we know when it's time to move beyond what we've already achieved and reach toward a new goal? How can we know when it's time to stretch ourselves (and our families) in order to broaden our tables?

There are two main answers to that question.

First, you should think about expanding your table when you cannot fulfill your assignment using your current resources. Meaning, you believe God is directing you to move in a specific direction or achieve a certain goal, but you don't have what it takes to reach that calling.

That often starts with financial resources. Let's say you feel convicted that God's assignment for your life includes purchasing a safe and reliable home for your family, but you simply don't have the money to make that purchase. Maybe you don't have the down payment, you don't have the right credit score, or you're already saddled with debt.

What should you do?

My answer would be to focus on expanding your table even as you trust God to provide what you need. That could mean seeking a new job or a second job. That could mean starting your own side hustle as we mentioned in a previous chapter. That could mean talking with your spouse about changing their income situation. Many options for making money exist when we take the time to seek them out.

Speaking generally, if you are having a difficult time fulfilling your God-given assignment because of a lack of money, it's likely that God is leading you to a place where He wants to expand the financial portion of your table. The question is, Will you be willing and flexible when the time comes for something big to change?

Importantly, expanding your table also includes the other elements of your table beyond money. Let's say part of your assignment is being a positive influence in the lives of young people in your community, and you've fulfilled that calling through coaching Little League sports. Then, as you move into your fifties, you don't have the energy you used to have. You can't move like you used to move. You're tired.

What are your options in that situation? One is to find a new way to fulfill your assignment, which may be the best option if your health is truly degenerating. But another option is to expand your table by investing more of your resources in your body. Find new doctors or a physical trainer. Work with a nutritionist to improve your diet.

My point is this: None of the resources that make up your table are static. They are flexible, which means they can be expanded or enhanced—if you are willing to take the necessary risks and make the necessary changes.

If you reach a point in life where you are unable to fulfill your assignment, it may be time to expand your table in a major way.

The second answer to the question—*When do I need to expand my table?*—is when you reach major landmarks or new stages in your life. You may need to expand your table when your life changes in a big or meaningful way. For example:

- You get married
- You have children
- You change jobs or move to a new area

- You have a major health need in your family (or even your extended family)
- You or a member of your family experience a major trauma
- Your children start college
- You have an empty nest
- You retire

Each of these big, important events presents an opportunity to take a step back and ask, "Am I able to handle this change with my current table?" If the answer is no, you likely need to expand that table by emphasizing or increasing one or more of the major resources you've been given.

Remember early in the book when I talked about the little wooden table my family set up in our dining room when I was a kid? We had to place it against the wall, which meant we couldn't even fit seats around the whole thing. It was a small table, but it fit our family's needs in that season; it did the trick when we were kids. Later, our family did get a bigger table that gave us more room to enjoy and interact with each other, which was important.

But what if my parents had said, "This little table has always worked in the past, so it will work for us now"? What if they had refused to expand their dining room table? As our family grew and matured, our interactions at that table would have become cramped and uncomfortable.

The same is true with our lives. Don't close off your table. Don't settle for what's comfortable or what you've always experienced. Instead, keep your table open. Be ready and willing to expand when the time is right.

Your Team Is Expandable

Okay, we've seen that part of managing the resources that make up your table is knowing when those resources need to be expanded. In the same way, being a good steward of your table means looking for opportunities to expand the team of people you invite to join you at your table and help you fulfill your assignment.

To review, you should never try to manage your table by yourself. Yes, you sit at the head of the table, which means you are the ultimate authority and decision-maker when it comes to your life. But it's a bad idea to try and manage those decisions using just your own brain and your own learning. Instead, you need to invite others who can offer wisdom and experience you don't have to join you at your table, thereby maximizing your table beyond your own ability.

That's critical, which is why I've been repeating that principle throughout these pages. Find people who can help you fulfill your assignment, and invite them to join you at your table.

But that raises an important question: *How many people should I have at my table? What's the right number of outside voices?*

There's no single answer to that question, mainly because every person is different. Each of us has a different assignment and a different table we're called to manage, so there are no cookie-cutter options when it comes to equipping our tables.

I will say this though: Your table needs to be effective. In other words, you will know you've got the right number of people at your table when you're able to function well, deal with problems, and make decisions efficiently. In the same way, you'll know you've got the wrong number of people at your table when you're not effective at fulfilling your assignment and moving your life in the direction it needs to go.

Let's dig a little deeper by answering two common questions.

First, how can you tell if you don't have enough people at your table? Answer: when you have a question or a problem and the people at your table don't know what to do—and don't even know how to figure out what to do.

Personally, I keep my table relatively small most of the time. I have invited six or seven people to speak regularly into my life and help me maximize my resources. When more than that many people are speaking into my life and offering varying guidance, I lose the ability to keep track of the different voices. I lose the effectiveness and efficiency that is so crucial to keeping things moving forward.

Even so, I have high expectations for my table. When I have a question that needs answering or a problem that needs solving, I bring it to my table. I talk things through with those people I have invited to be part of my life in that way. In doing so, I expect those people will be able to answer my question, or at the very least point me in the direction of the answer or solution I need.

When that doesn't happen—when nobody at my table can answer my question—then I know it's time to expand. It's time to bring in someone new to help me in that specific area.

Second, how can you tell when you have too many people at your table? Answer: when you have a hard time managing all the voices speaking into your life—especially when trying to navigate those voices becomes stressful or causes you to feel anxious.

You may also sense a problem when the voices at your table are pushing you to move in different directions or giving completely opposite answers to important questions. Meaning, if someone at your table encourages you to marry a person, but another individual believes that person is completely wrong for you—that's a problem. The same is true if one voice at your table is guiding you to leave your career and start your own business, while another voice is emphatically saying you need a long-term plan for promotion and retirement at your current job.

Let me make sure I communicate this well, because I don't want you to have a group of yes-men at your table. You don't want a bunch of people who all think the same things and say the same things. That's not helpful. You need people with different ideas and different experiences speaking into your life. You want to develop a healthy conversation.

But when people know you well, care about you, and have a good understanding of your assignment, rarely will those people form completely opposite opinions about your life's direction. When it comes to the key issues that connect with your assignment, there should be a general consensus among those you invite to join you at your table.

If not though—if two or more people keep pushing you to move in clearly different directions—then you likely have too many voices. Someone needs to go. (More on that in a moment.)

The basic principle I am teaching in this chapter is that the

You need
people with
different ideas
and different
experiences
speaking into
your life.

resources that make up your table are not static and should be able to flex—and the same is true for the team of people you invite into your life to help you manage and maximize those resources. So let me conclude by offering two more important concepts that can help you remain flexible and navigate the ups and downs with the people joining you at your table.

TAKE ADVANTAGE OF SEASONAL RELATIONSHIPS

Take a moment and visualize the table at your home. I'm talking about the one in your dining room or kitchen—the place where you eat your meals. It goes without saying that certain people will always have access to that table, right? Some people in your life possess an open invitation to join you every time you sit down for a meal.

If you have a spouse and children, they are the main examples of people who always have access. Or maybe you live with your parents, and you are the one who has an open seat to join their table for most meals. Or maybe one of those neighbor kids is always at your place, and you've just developed a rhythm where that kid knows they can join your family for a meal whenever they'd like.

My point is, some people have a permanent place at your table.

Now imagine yourself inviting someone over for dinner one night. A friend or a coworker. Maybe someone from your extended family. They come and enjoy a good steak and potatoes. Fresh salad. Some kind of artisanal bread with real butter. Pie and ice cream for dessert. They love it. They have a wonderful time. Who wouldn't?

But what if that person shows up at your house the next night, ready for another meal? Then breakfast the following morning? Then dinner again?

Wouldn't that be weird? Wouldn't it be strange for someone to assume that being invited to your table for one meal meant they possessed an open invitation to eat at your table whenever they liked?

Yep, that would be super weird, and I bet you can already see the point I want to make. Just because you invite someone to your table for a specific purpose or a specific season does not mean you should feel pressured or obligated to keep them at your table for the rest of your life.

In other words, sometimes people join your table for a time. They take a seasonal seat at your table to help with a specific issue, and then they move back out again.

That's what happened with the sales coach I described at the beginning of this chapter. During the six months when he taught me how to sell, you'd better believe he had a seat at my table. He was at my right hand, working with me just about every day. I asked for his advice and insight on a whole bunch of issues that touched my table, and I was grateful to hear his thoughts not only on how to sell video courses but also on the entire direction and purpose of my business. He had a major seat at my table for those six months.

But then, once that season was over and we successfully launched *The Single's Blueprint*, he hopped out of that chair and moved away from my table.

That doesn't mean I ended our relationship or burned the bridge that connected us. No, we stayed friends, and we are still friends to this day. In fact, whenever we launch a new course as part of Anthony O'Neal Enterprises, I invite him back to the table to help make sure we are doing things right in terms of selling my vision morally and spiritually. He joins us for a time, and then he vacates the table once more.

Just like me, you need to make seasonal seats available at your table. These are opportunities for individuals or groups to come into your life for a specific period of time in order to accomplish a specific goal. You need to keep your table open enough and flexible enough for those types of relationships.

Here are some examples of what a seasonal seat might look like at your table:

- You and your fiancée spend several weeks seeing a therapist or a pastor for premarital counseling.
- You hire someone to help you learn the basics of marketing and search engine optimization (SEO) to boost the performance of your YouTube channel.
- You find someone to help you polish your Spanish before you spend a summer traveling through Central America.
- You hire a writer to help you produce a bestselling book (shout out to you, Sam!).
- You seek out a nutritionist to help you plan a healthier diet so you can lose weight.

I could offer you many more examples, but I'm sure several have already come to mind for your specific situation. I want to say it plainly: These relationships are good and helpful. They are an important part of stewarding your table well.

So you should definitely make some seasonal seats available at your table. Just don't forget the "seasonal" part.

MAKE SURE YOUR SEATS HAVE WHEELS

My final piece of advice when it comes to maintaining an open and flexible table is to mentally put wheels on the chairs that surround your table.

What do I mean? Two things, but they both revolve around the same idea: You don't want the seats around your table to be locked in place. Instead, you want them to be movable and adjustable. You should be able to modify those seats in two specific ways.

First, it will be helpful at times to switch around the people at your table in terms of their importance and influence in your life.

Let's say you have a mentor who is the primary advisor in your life. You turn to this person when you need to discuss the most important questions or issues in your life—your marriage, your health, your career choices, and so on. I imagine that person sitting at your right hand at your table. They have the place of honor. That mentor's voice is the one you seek out and listen for most often, so you keep them close.

That's a good and natural arrangement—to make sure your best advisors are closest to you.

But a moment will come when you need to switch things around. Maybe you're in the middle of a financial crisis, for example, and you need to spend a lot of time seeking wisdom and guidance from your financial advisor. If that's the case, I recommend you metaphorically roll your mentor farther down the table and bring your financial person closest to you for that season. Don't feel like you have to seek out financial advice from your mentor just because that person is usually closest to you.

That's why I say the seats around your table need wheels. Reserve the freedom to arrange your table in whatever way will serve you best for that specific season. And then, when another issue comes up or you have another season focused on a specific need, rearrange your table again so the people you encounter most and spend the most time with are those who have the most expertise in that area of concern.

Second, those seats need wheels because a moment will come when you need to roll people away from your table. At times you will need to remove people from your table, and you don't want those seats to be bolted to the floor. You want them to roll in easily when needed and then roll out again when that need is no longer there.

What does it look like to remove someone from your table? In my experience, it means being both honest and direct: "Thank you so much for everything you've done to help me with [fill in the blank]. It's been great."

This is especially important for those seasonal seats at your table. The worst thing you can do is let people linger or keep them hanging around. Because very soon your table will become cluttered and hard to manage, with too many voices and too many opinions.

In the same way you need to verbally invite people to join your table, you should also verbally thank them and make it clear the time has come for them to move out of your inner circle. There's no need to be rude. There's no need to be abrasive or sharp. Just express your appreciation for their contribution, and let them know you'll be in touch the next time you need their counsel.

A few years back an extended family member was working as one of my team members. She started working remotely, but it eventually became clear that I needed her to join our team at the office in order for all of us to be most productive. When I made that request, however, she told me honestly that she could not move to Maryland because of her daughter's school.

I understood. She had to make the decision that was right for her family, and I respected her for choosing to care for her daughter in that way.

"You're still my family," I told her, "but we will need to end this working relationship." I thanked her for the ways she had contributed to our company, and I gave her three months' salary as a severance package because I love her and wanted to honor her—but when I officially ended our working relationship, I removed her from my table.

Unfortunately, people don't always take the hint or agree to relinquish their place at the table of our lives. They keep acting as if they have been invited to offer guidance or advice, even after we have removed them from our tables.

In those circumstances, the best response is still to be honest and direct: "I appreciate you wanting to help me out, but I need to be clear with you that I have other people in my life I rely on to advise me on this subject." Those conversations can be uncomfortable, I know. They can be messy. But they're also necessary.

Whether you are inviting someone to join your table or inviting them to leave, be open about their place in your life. Tell them how you see your relationship and what you hope to receive from them. Then move forward in confidence as the head of your table.

CHAPTER 10

THE IMPORTANCE OF A MESSY TABLE

It's time for Thanksgiving dinner, but not the kind of Thanksgiving I would make for just myself. I'm talking about a real meal. A real event. Multiple grandmothers have been working for days to get everything ready for this incredible celebration.

Can you see it all arranged there on the table? Two main dishes: a roasted turkey on one side and a glazed ham on the other. Both cooked to perfection. (There's a BBQ turkey still in the kitchen as a reserve.) The rest of the table is packed with just about every side dish you can think of. Mashed potatoes. Sweet potato casserole with those caramelized marshmallows on top. Corn bread dressing. Green beans. Black-eyed peas. Yellow corn. Green salad. Potato salad. Macaroni and cheese. Deviled eggs with paprika on top. Cranberry sauce still in the shape of a can. Fried apples. Corn bread and yeast rolls and crescent rolls. Saucers filled with gravy. Cups filled with punch.

It's all there. It's all glorious. It's all ready to eat!

If you've been to one of those types of celebrations, you know what happens next. Dad or Grandpa leads the table in prayer, and then everyone dives in. Plates are passed around and loaded up. Platters are passed around and emptied out. An hour of chewing and chatting and laughing goes by. Someone eventually falls asleep at the table, but everyone else keeps going.

"Pass the mashed potatoes."

"Who's got the corn bread?"

"Mom, can I have some of that punch?"

Just when everyone is starting to think they can't eat another bite, Grandma brings out the pies. Pumpkin pie. Rhubarb pie. Pecan pie. And tubs of vanilla ice cream.

Turns out everyone has a little room left after all, and they dig in again.

Eventually someone gets up and starts to clear the table, and others join to help. Dishes in the sink. Platters and pans stacked along the counter. Cups tucked in wherever they can fit.

Now try to imagine what that table would look like after such a meal. Imagine the tablecloth. Crumbs all over. Gravy stains. Bits of different types of food spilling over to the floor. A big wet puddle where one of the kids spilled their drink and their mom tried to mop it up with a napkin.

Can you see that table in your mind? It's a mess. And it should be a mess. Right?

In fact, if I were to walk into someone's home after Thanksgiving dinner and see a clean table with a clean tablecloth and no mess on the floor, I would be suspicious. I would assume it must not have been a successful meal.

Why? Because when it comes to food, a delicious table is a messy table! When you've got a lot of food and a lot of people laughing and enjoying themselves, things are going to get a little untidy.

In a similar way, when it comes to our lives, an effective table is a messy table. That's what I want to focus on in this chapter.

An effective
table is a
messy table.

Learn to Live with the Mess

As we start working through this final chapter together, I think it's helpful to remember the main theme of this book. Namely, you have been given a table, which is your life. You have been given many wonderful resources—a spiritual health, mental health, physical health, meaningful work, financial resources, relationships, and more—all of which you are supposed to manage and steward. That process of taking control of your resources is what I call taking a seat at the head of your table.

Importantly, though, we don't sit at the head of our tables simply to be comfortable or to be in charge. We are stewards. We have been called by our Creator to manage those resources in a way that makes a difference in the lives of others and in our world, and we do that by using our resources to fulfill our assignments—our God-given purposes.

Now, having said all that, here's the main principle I want to communicate as we wrap up this book together: You can't make a difference without making a mess.

That's true in our personal lives as we seek to grow and mature and change. That's true in our families. That's true in our workplaces. That's true in our communities, in our cities, and even across the world. When we invest our resources well, we're going to change things. We're going to change people. We're going to make an impact.

And you can't make an impact without making a mess.

The more I have gone out into the world to visit clients and meet with other professionals, the more I've discovered what I can learn about a person by looking at their office. Specifically, I can learn a lot about the way a person works (and the amount that person works) by just a quick glance around their workspace, and especially their desk.

The people I know who work the hardest usually have the messiest offices. I don't mean "messy" in terms of trash spilled on the floor or grimy chairs or that kind of thing. I mean messy in the sense of being well used. The successful people I know typically don't work in pristine environments. Stacks of paper are piled on desk corners. A couple of used coffee mugs might be resting on tables or piled in the sink. Notes are scribbled here and there, or whiteboards are covered with goals and strategies written out in different colors.

I know that's true of my office. I used to make a promise to myself after each visit from the cleaners: *This time I will keep things just as clean as they are now. I'm not going to let any messes accumulate.*

Nope. Two days later, the office is back to normal. Back to untidy. Because I use that space for real work, and real work is messy.

I say all that because I want you to understand that sitting at the head of your table and investing in fulfilling your assignment will be a messy business. Some stuff will make you feel untidy—maybe even a little uncomfortable. And some situations will need to be cleaned up.

Here are two big examples of what I mean when I say you must learn to live with some mess if you want your table to be effective.

MESSY CONVERSATIONS

In every chapter of this book, I have encouraged you to invite good, talented, healthy, mature people to your table—people who understand your assignment and can help you maximize your resources with good direction and good advice. That is a necessary part of stewarding your table in a way that makes a difference.

Yet I also need to make it clear that inviting good, strong people to offer advice and direction in your life will generate lots of conversation. *Lots* of conversation. When you've got the right people around your table, most of that conversation will be healthy and helpful. But it won't be neat and tidy. When you encourage people to tell you the truth, they will inevitably say things that make you feel uncomfortable. Maybe even offended.

In other words, inviting people to join you at the table of your life means you will need to have some messy conversations.

One time a few years back, we launched a video course that was incredibly successful right out of the gate. We earned more than $100,000 in revenue within the first few hours of the course going live. In fact, we had sales piling up so quickly that the company that handles our payments became suspicious. That company actually froze our account to run a quick investigation and make sure we weren't doing anything fraudulent. (We weren't, and the company got us back online relatively quickly.)

When that first happened, I sent out a group text to my team members: "Hey, guys, just wanted to let everyone know that Stripe has frozen our accounts. I'm working on it and hope to have some resolution soon."

Pretty quickly I got a text back on that string from one of my team members: "Am I still getting paid?"

Whoa. For some reason, that text really hit me the wrong way in that moment. I felt upset. Maybe even a little angry. At that point this guy had been with me for more than two years.

So I called him up. And we had what I would describe as a messy conversation.

When he answered the phone, I told him what was on my mind. "Bro, what's with this text? Have I ever missed a paycheck for you?" I told him I was disappointed to hear him express that kind of doubt in a stressful moment, especially on a group text with the entire team. I told him I wished his attitude had been more along the lines of "What can I do to help?" or "How can I pitch in?"

He heard me. He understood what I was saying. But he also expressed what he was thinking. Mainly, that he was a husband and a father. He had responsibilities and wanted to know if having our accounts frozen would impact salaries—and if so, would that impact be for a short time or a long time? He *needed* that information because he needed to communicate with his wife and let her know if there would be a disruption in their finances.

Okay, I thought. *Okay.*

I heard him. I understood where he was coming from. We kept talking. We kept being honest. That conversation was uncomfortable from start to finish because it was *real* from start to finish. It was genuine. It was important. And it allowed us to reach resolution rather than let something fester underneath the surface of our relationship for weeks or months or years.

Messy conversations are necessary for strong relationships. (Just ask anyone who's married.) And as we saw a few chapters ago, strong relationships are necessary for a strong table.

Now, you might be nodding your head at this moment and thinking, *I agree with that. I'll have to deal with messy conversations if I want to be effective at managing my table.* That's good. That's true.

But that's not all.

Sitting at the head of your table means you will also have to *initiate* messy conversations—which can be difficult. After all, it's one thing to allow those conversations to develop around you, and yet another to join in and offer your opinion. It's a whole different thing to be the one who picks up the phone.

I've had to develop that discipline in my life in order to steward my table well. I'm not someone who enjoys conflict. I don't like being involved in drama. But I've learned that initiating a difficult conversation is much better and much healthier than ignoring something harmful in the present that will grow more and more harmful in the future.

For example, just recently I was talking with Stephen Chandler when he said something that struck me hard. It hurt. Even at the time, I didn't think he meant to hurt me, but that didn't change the fact that it hurt. So I knew I needed to address it.

"Whoa, whoa," I said. "Bro, I don't like the way you said that just now." And I explained why.

He listened to me. He heard me, and he thought about it for a minute. "You're right, man," he said. "I apologize. I shouldn't have phrased things that way."

"Okay, cool," I said. "Thank you. You got time to play nine holes?"

That was it. Moment over. Crisis resolved, and no grudges retained. We just moved forward.

That's important to remember as well: Messy conversations don't have to be long conversations. They just need to be honest.

Which reminds me: You need to cultivate honesty with the people who sit around your table. Encourage honest sharing and healthy conversations—even healthy disagreements. The goal is for the people at your table to offer their wisdom and their experience and their direction without holding back. Then you as the head of the table can make the final decisions.

So you don't need yes-men at your table. You need people who are willing to disagree with you. You need people who are willing to challenge you—even to argue with you.

When those things can be done under the umbrella of mutual respect, you will have a happy, healthy, messy table that makes a real difference in the world.

MESSY MISTAKES

As I said earlier, sitting at the head of your table means the buck stops with you. After you've gathered all the information and participated in a healthy (and messy) conversation about an issue or a problem, you are the one who makes the final decision. You are the one who chooses how to resolve that issue or solve that problem.

Which means you will inevitably lead your table into more than a few missteps. You *will* slip up. Guaranteed. No doubt about it.

When you truly sit at the head of your table, you're going to make some mistakes. Even some big mistakes. And that's okay.

I made my biggest mistake not that long ago. We were recording one of my podcasts, and I was talking about some of my goals for raising kids one day. I said I want to travel the world with my kids when they are young. I want to take them to Europe. I want to take them to Israel and open the Bible as a living textbook. And I want to take my kids to Africa to show them the many cultures and many different types of environments and ecosystems on that continent.

Okay, that's what I *meant* to say. What I actually said was that I wanted to show my kids the motherland where people are "staying in woods and trees."

Ouch. Right? In the context of the whole podcast, it was clear that I was talking about exposing my future children to many different cultures and environments because those different places matter. That sentiment was clear to me. It was clear to my team members. Even in the editing stages of the podcast, nobody put their hand up to say, "Anthony, this could be offensive to some people." We thought the context made everything clear.

But the context wasn't included in a clip. And that single clip made it seem as if I think people in Africa are swinging around in trees rather than living in houses and neighborhoods and cities.

And the clip went viral. It blew up.

The day after that podcast went live, I came online to an explosion of people from all over the world sending hate my way. Laughing at me. Tearing into me. Criticizing me in every way possible. Man, it was crazy! For several days that week, I was the number one trending topic in Africa. #AnthonyOneal was all over Instagram, TikTok, and X (Twitter at the time), and not in a good way.

Beyond the embarrassment, our company took a major hit from that whole incident. We lost about twenty thousand audience members across our different platforms, which is a big deal. A huge loss both in terms of finance and influence.

So yeah, I have plenty of experience with failure. With mistakes. When you step up to sit at the head of your table, you'll gain plenty of experience in those areas as well. It comes with the territory. That's the bad news.

The good news is that most of our mistakes have temporary consequences. When we handle them well, they don't linger for long, and they can help us learn valuable lessons that make us more effective for the future.

What does it mean to handle mistakes well? Three things:

1. Own it. When you make a decision or do something that ends up being a mistake, take ownership of that decision. Don't run away from it. Accept your mistake both internally (to yourself) and externally (to others).

2. Apologize. When you make a mistake that directly impacts or wounds other people, be quick to apologize to those people. I'm not talking about one of those vague apologies either, such as, "If anyone took offense at what I said, I apologize." Nope. That's not it.

   Real apologies are personal and specific. "Hey, man, I know what I did was hurtful to you because it [fill in the

Most of our
mistakes have
temporary
consequences.

blank] and made you feel [fill in the blank]. And I want to say I was wrong. I am sorry."

3. Avoid excuses. There's a little word that can cause big problems when you're trying to apologize. It's the word *but*. "I'm so sorry. What I did was wrong, and I know it hurt you. *But . . .*" Nope again!

When you own a mistake and apologize for the consequences of that mistake, you can undercut all your efforts at resolution by making excuses for that mistake. By justifying your actions. So don't do it. Own your mistake. Apologize for your mistake. And don't try to go a little easier on yourself by tossing out a bunch of excuses. Just move forward.

I'm grateful I was able to follow those steps after my Africa failure. When everything was swirling and chaotic in the days following that podcast, I did everything I could to show that I owned my words. I didn't run away from them. Instead, I made a video to apologize to the people of Africa and others around the world who were hurt by what I'd said. I acknowledged the hurt, and I expressed the disappointment I felt in myself for my words. I also apologized to my team members for the way my statement reflected on them, and even for the financial uncertainty that came about afterward.

No trying to clarify this or that. No explaining. No excuses. We just moved forward with our work, and I moved forward with my table and my assignment.

I said earlier that mistakes can be positive when they teach us new things, so what lesson did I learn from that experience?

That the *intent* behind my words doesn't mitigate the *impact* of those words. I had hurt people, and the fact that I never meant to hurt them didn't make things any better. I learned I had to deal with the reality of what occurred rather than try to focus on what I wish had happened or what I had intended to happen.

Again, mistakes are messy. They are uncomfortable. But they are also inevitable. So don't run from them. Do learn from them. And do move forward as a more experienced steward of your table.

Learn to Be Your Authentic Self

So much of our modern world pushes us to connect success with perfection. We're told in a bunch of different ways that a perfect life is possible when we are successful.

You see this on commercials all the time. Like the one where two attractive spouses living in a suburban mansion with two attractive kids buy each other luxury cars wrapped in huge red bows for Christmas. You see it in magazines and paparazzi photos. You see it everywhere on social media. People posting in their bathing suits from the spa or the beach or fancy resorts located in faraway countries. Or the silly "woke up like this" selfies. Or those who post choreographed casual poses from expensive restaurants.

When you keep getting exposed to that kind of nonsense, it's easy to start believing perfection is possible. Not only that, it's easy to start thinking perfection is *expected*.

I trust by now you recognize the lie in those who are pushing us toward perfection. I hope you've seen even in this chapter that we can't achieve perfection and be effective in managing our tables. Why? Because effectiveness is messy.

So let go of perfection. It's a silly and unreachable goal. Instead, aim for a life of authenticity. In my opinion, that is the best possible gift you can give yourself.

What do I mean by *authenticity*? It's the ability to be the person you were created to be. No posturing. No pretending. No trying to figure out what other people expect you to do or think or say. Just you living as you.

One of the most important decisions I ever made in my life was choosing to be Anthony Bernard O'Neal all the time. To be myself and nobody else every minute of every day. I wish I could describe the freedom that has come with that choice—not to mention wellness and abundance.

I want the same for you.

I haven't written this book to tell you that being a good steward of your table is easy, because it's not. It's difficult. It takes diligence, discipline, and determination.

I haven't written this book to tell you that managing your table will keep things neat and tidy, because it won't. If you use your table to fulfill your assignment and make a difference in the lives of other people, you'll make some messes. You'll have to manage difficult conversations and clean up after mistakes. Both will happen. So get your bib on.

I haven't even written this book to tell you that you're guaranteed to succeed and that your life will definitely be filled with abundance and wellness and freedom—because I don't know what choices you'll make or what God has in store for your future.

No, I have written this book because a major part of *my* assignment is helping other people improve their lives. That is one of the reasons God has placed me on this planet, and that is my primary goal in producing these pages.

I want you to succeed. I want you to experience the gifts of abundance and wellness and freedom, just like I have. I really do believe you can receive those gifts and so much more when you make the active, intentional decision to manage your table well—to sit at the head of your table and set your sights on investing all of those resources into achieving your God-given assignment. It really can happen.

At this point, though, I have been faithful in my job. In my assignment. I have offered what I know and what I believe to the best of my ability.

The question is, Where will you go from here?

ACKNOWLEDGMENTS

Six years ago I sat down with nothing but a microphone, one light (that wasn't enough for a Black man), and a dream that was larger than life itself. I didn't even have a name for my show yet, but I knew I wanted to empower people to escape debt, build wealth, and reclaim control of their destinies. That first recording session sparked a feeling deep within me—a premonition that this journey was going to be monumental, that it would bless many lives. As I reflect on this journey, the reality is even more profound than I imagined. What started as an episode aired to ten thousand subscribers has blossomed into a robust community of over a million and now, miraculously, a book.

To every member of the E3 community, who perhaps didn't fully know what they were signing up for but dove in headfirst nonetheless, this book is a testament to our collective courage to occupy the head of the table, to boldly step into the lives we are destined to live.

From the inception of *The Table with Anthony O'Neal*,

your enthusiasm and support have been my cornerstone. To those who have faced doubts, including myself, and those who questioned what was to love about my show, it was in those moments of doubt that my resolve solidified and my purpose was clarified.

To my parents, Anthony and Terry Ross and John and Ann Givens, your unwavering faith in me has been my foundation. Your sacrifices have not gone unnoticed, and the love and lessons you've imparted have shaped me into the man I am today. To my siblings, Yvette Henry and John Givens, your unique strengths and contributions to the world continue to inspire me.

A special thanks to my core team at the Neatness Network—CJ Nurse, Alex Lewis, Michelle Morris, Danni Roseman, and Rebecca Patterson. From the earliest days, your commitment to excellence has propelled this dream into reality. Your patience and perseverance have not only supported this venture but have also pushed us to reach higher.

I am profoundly grateful to my pastors and best friends, Stephen and Zai Chandler, and the Union Church community. Your guidance has been a beacon in my life, encouraging me not only to grow but also to thrive surrounded by love and support.

To my friends—Dharius Daniels, Keion Henderson, Brian Bullock, Amy Porterfield, Jeremy Wright, Jamal Miller, Mignon Francois, Todd Galberth, and Glen Henry—who have been my pillars during one of the most challenging transitional periods of my life. Whether over long phone calls or face-to-face meetings, your wisdom, prayers, and unwavering support have profoundly impacted both my life and the direction of my company. Your readiness to assist at any moment has truly helped guide my path forward. Thank you for being there when I needed you the most.

To my future wife—at the time of writing this book, I have not met you, but I can't wait to deeply love, protect, and cover you. Every decision I've made in the last three years has been with you and our future family in mind. There is already room at the head of my table waiting for you, and I can't wait to share it with you and create a space and place for you to flourish.

Above all, I thank God for His endless grace and mercy. I am a flawed man who has been blessed immeasurably more than I deserve. My commitment to building a legacy of wealthy kingdom men and women remains unwavering. I am humbled and grateful for every blessing, every challenge, and every victory on this journey.

This book, this journey, is for all of us. Here's to taking our rightful place at the head of the table, to living the lives we were destined for, and to the continued blessing that comes from daring to dream big.

NOTES

CHAPTER 1: DEFINING YOUR TABLE

1. Dharius Daniels, *Your Purpose Is Calling: Your Difference Is Your Destiny* (Zondervan, 2022), 20.

CHAPTER 4: MENTAL WELLNESS

1. National Institute of Mental Health, "Statistics," National Institutes of Health, accessed December 15, 2023, https://www.nimh.nih.gov/health/statistics.
2. A. M. Williamson and Anne-Marie Feyer, "Moderate Sleep Deprivation Produces Impairments in Cognitive and Motor Performance Equivalent to Legally Prescribed Levels of Alcohol Intoxication," *Occupational and Environmental Medicine* 57, no. 10 (October 2000): 649–55, https://www.ncbi.nlm.nih.gov/pmc/articles/PMC1739867/pdf/v057p00649.pdf.

CHAPTER 5: PHYSICAL WELLNESS

1. National Institute of Diabetes and Digestive and Kidney Diseases, "Overweight and Obesity Statistics," National Institutes of Health, accessed December 28, 2022, https://www.niddk.nih.gov/health-information/health-statistics/overweight-obesity.

2. National Institute of Diabetes and Digestive and Kidney Diseases, "Overweight and Obesity Statistics."

3. "Cigarette Smoking in the U.S.," Centers for Disease Control and Prevention, accessed June 25, 2024, https://www.cdc.gov/tobacco /data_statistics/fact_sheets/fast_facts/cigarette-smoking-in-the-us .html.

4. "Statistics About Diabetes," American Diabetes Association, accessed December 28, 2022, https://diabetes.org/about-diabetes /statistics/about-diabetes.

5. National Heart, Lung, and Blood Institute, "What Are Sleep Deprivation and Deficiency?," National Institutes of Health, accessed December 28, 2022, https://www.nhlbi.nih.gov/health /sleep-deprivation.

6. Selena Simmons-Duffin, "'Live Free and Die?' The Sad State of U.S. Life Expectancy," National Public Radio, March 25, 2023, https://www.npr.org/sections/health-hots/2023/03/25/1164819944 /live-free-and-die-the-sad-state-of-u-s-life-expectancy.

CHAPTER 6: A HEALTHY CAREER

1. Grand View Research, Inc., "Digital Content Creation Market to Hit $69.8 Billion by 2030: Grand View Research, Inc.," PR Newswire, March 28, 2023, https://www.prnewswire.com/news -releases/digital-content-creation-market-to-hit-69-8-billion-by -2030-grand-view-research-inc-301783632.html.

2. Mike Florio, "NFL National Revenue Reaches $11.98 Billion in 2022," NBC Sports: Pro Football Talk, July 19, 2023, https:// www.nbcsports.com/nfl/profootballtalk/rumor-mill/news /nfl-national-revenue-reaches-11-98-billion-in-2022.

CHAPTER 7: FINANCIAL WELLNESS

1. Lucas Wisenthal et al., "25 Iconic Quotes About Money," Complex, October 29, 2021, https://www.complex.com/life/a /lucas-wisenthal/iconic-money-quotes.

2. "What Oprah Learned from Jim Carrey | Oprah's Life Class | Oprah Winfrey Network," posted by Oprah Winfrey Network

(OWN) on October 13, 2011, YouTube video, 1:53, https://www .youtube.com/watch?v=nPU5bjzLZX0.

3. "I Think Everybody Should Get Rich and Famous So They Can See That That's Not the Answer," Quote Investigator, November 9, 2022, https://quoteinvestigator.com/2022/11/09/rich-famous/.

4. Jaspreet Singh (@MinorityM1ndset), "Money isn't everything. But, the lack of money can destroy everything," X, January 3, 2024, 1:09 p.m., https://x.com/MinorityM1ndset/status /1742624300291719630.

5. Rob Berger, "Top 100 Money Quotes of All Time," *Forbes*, updated April 14, 2022, https://www.forbes.com/sites/robertberger /2014/04/30/top-100-money-quotes-of-all-time/?sh=5ce16b4c4998.

CHAPTER 8: RELATIONAL WELLNESS

1. Michele Majidi, "Number of Close Friends Had by Adults in the United States in 1990 and 2021," Statista, January 13, 2023, https://www.statista.com/statistics/1358672/number-of-close -friends-us-adults/.

2. Alexa Mikhail, "Loneliness Is a Health Crisis Comparable to Smoking Up to 15 Cigarettes a Day. Here's How to Combat It," *Fortune*, June 15, 2023, https://fortune.com/well/2023/06/15 /loneliness-comparable-to-smoking-up-to-15-cigarettes-a-day/.

ABOUT THE AUTHOR

Anthony O'Neal is the number one national bestselling author of *Debt-Free Degree*, a personal finance expert, and the host of the popular podcast and YouTube show *The Table*. Since 2014 he has challenged cultural norms and equipped millions of people to live a debt-free life, break generational wealth gaps, and build true wealth. He has appeared on *Good Morning America*, *Live with Kelly and Mark*, *Fox and Friends*, *Rachael Ray*, *Tamron Hall*, and CNN and has been featured in *Success Magazine*, MarketWatch, *Bloomberg*, *Black Enterprise*, and GOBankingRates, among others.

In 2023 alone his show received over 18.7 million views and 5.3 million downloads, empowering people to achieve financially successful futures. Anthony is a sought-after, dynamic public speaker, addressing audiences of over forty thousand people. He was recognized in *Black Enterprise*'s 2023 40 Under 40 list and *Success Magazine*'s "25 Personal and Professional Development Influencers to Follow."

Anthony resides in the Washington, DC, suburbs. You can connect with him on Instagram, YouTube, TikTok, Twitter, Facebook, and at AnthonyONeal.com.